AKANSHA PUBLISHING HOUSE
4649-B/21, Ansari Road
Darya Ganj, New Delhi - 110 002
Email: ektabooks@yahoo.com
Ph.: 23263193/9811582579
Fax: 011-23263193

CONTEMPORARY NAGA SOCIAL FORMATIONS AND ETHNIC IDENTITY

First Published 2006

ISBN 81-8370-064-0

[The responsibility for the facts stated, conclusions reached etc., is entirely that of the Authors. The publisher is not responsible for them, whatsoever.]

PRINTED IN INDIA

Published by M.P. Misra for Akansha Publishing House, New Delhi and Printed at Aryan Enterprises, Delhi

CONTENTS.

FOREWORD

The North-East of India in terms of area amounts to a tiny 8% of the total national canvas while in terms of population, it merely amounts to 3.75% of the national count (2001 Census). Despite its miniscule size, the region have qualified itself to be a source of national concern of immense proportions. It represents issues to be resolved, understood and treated. Most of these are steeped in their social history, convoluting into political, economic and cultural ulcers of articulation and movement there-of, many coalescing into ethnic outburst and sub-national claims of demanding reforms amendments and justice, while some mobilises into separatist independence pursuits.

Reflecting on the above most communities of the region relate to one or the other facet of issues mentioned. For many, current focus upon their situation would be simply an exercise of studying ongoing issues begun in the past. Conversely a discussion on the Naga tribesmen of Nagaland state would aptly fit into the frame – although in this case, it is not a discussion of Naga history, nor a political examination of Naga politics. It is simply a sociological examination from the frame of change – of traditional Naga socio-structural inequality to contemporary social formations of class divisions, largely from a conceptual point. It is an attempt at understanding how exogenous forces can trigger endogenous currents within communities toward change. It is a combination of old and new updated data as in a continuum.

Thus, this effort is an exercise in non-historical retrospection so to speak on some past Naga social processes finally arriving on some select contemporary issues of the Naga social structure, aimed at generating a level of non-emotive introspection. It is based upon a stand and principal of a long ago doctoral effort, where in the serious consideration of Naga ethos and pathos, a question is posed as to whether their contemporary situation is a case of development or decay.

For most readers, the contents of this effort will not be new nor worth the consideration. It is only hoped that many of the issues and concepts herein, may inspire regional scholars in the further in-depth study of their communities and in particular Naga scholars for whom current in-state situations should impel them to attempts of understanding their background in greater magnitude as to enable them to digest real-time developments in clearer perspectives and thus further their academic resonance.

IMO LANUTEMJIN AIER

North Eastern Hill University
Shillong 2006

CHAPTER-I

INTRODUCTION

The study is addressed to emerging class characteristics as a case of social transformation of discrete tribal communities fused into a larger Naga society inhabiting the eastern most part of the Indian union. Such a transformation may be traced from the time of the British colonial rule in the 19th century on the Nagas and after 1947, of their social encounter with the larger Indian society. The contemporary Naga social formation is largely as a consequence of being subjected to certain exogenous forces, identified with the intrusion of the colonial rule. These forces are Identified with: (i) imposition of administrative/political control over the various tribes; (ii) proselytization of the tribals into Christianity; (iii) introduction of formal education; (iv) monetization of the economy; and (v) growth of rural/urban market centres. As a consequence to these, some indogenous forces of change came into being, which may be identified with: (i) towns as service network; (ii) breakdown of tribal communal feelings; (iii) shift to new occupations; (iv) urban achievement orientation, and (v) urban centres as an arena of a new type of more sophisticated politics. Rooted in the social consequences of the above, Naga ethnicity found expression as early as 1918 with the Naga club. Such an ethnic expression in political tones was further compounded, for in as much the colonial rule generated it, it also implied in later historical phase, an encounter with the larger Indian society, a process which was fraught with fears and uncertainty for the Naga tribals.

Politically, matters were intensified as to the Naga tribals being already an integral part of the Indian nation state and society, finding expression in a claim that they were considered a unit to the arrangements of independence after British rule. As against this background, the Naga claims were in contradiction. With such controversy, Naga tribal reactions in political terms were unleashed in pursuance of their own perceived 'nationalistic' objectives. This, in consequence only fanned their tribal spirit and ethnic identity. In relation to the emerging Indian nation state at large, it assumed the appearance of an intricate interplay of the conflicting aspirations of the Indian core and the Naga periphery. In the aftermath of the claims, counter-claims, controversies, insurgency and reprisal, a respite materialized in 1963, through which the Nagas could join the Indian Nation state as a federating unit known as Nagaland. It involved a political agreement, i.e. Article 371 A, granting large measures of autonomy to the Nagas as a constitutional sanction. For this political factor, the Naga ethnicity got itself sanctioned vis-à-vis the larger Indian Union and the Indian social structure. Through this arrangement, the Nagas received profuse special favours and attention, that began a relationship of paternalism on one, and on the other, depemdent conditioning. Sociologically, it may explain the Nagas' contemporary ethnic expression in terms of regional reflections and on the other hand, a failure to concretely relate and identify themselves with the Indian Union. This predicament is further compounded by pursuance of political independent identity outside the Indian Union by some sections of the Naga society that began with the Naga National Council (N.N.C.) and the National Socialist Council of Nagaland (N.S.C.N.).

Prospectively, for the above reasons, added to the national

plan of rapid economic development for the tribals, vast economic aid is being poured into Nagaland after independence. It appears that the Nagaland was not prepared for such large scale monetary inpourings. Least of all Naga economic development, the central monetary aids have brought several serious consequences. For one, it explains the emergence of certain neo-elites and symptoms of class characteristics, mainly as a consequence of certain mechanisms of anomaly in distribution of the monetary assistance, conspicously placed against the major rural backdrop of underdevelopment. A serious development took place in such a situation when the traditional Naga economy largely of cultivation,lost its autonomy and became a dependent and integral part of the complex Indian economic structure. It is this phenomenon, which may explain for the contemporary lack of "inner motivation" within the Nagas to be self generative , so much so that it is an established criticism that they now view themselves as a "sponsored society". All these have resulted into a situation in which Nagaland is in the process of being economically peripheral to the Indian social core and its metropolitan capital intensive economy. The same largely describes the entire situation of the North-East as well.

The Framework of Social Formation

The study of social formation identifies society in a state of dynamics – with corresponding establishment of reciprocal relations between its social and political institutions, the structure being determined by the state of the economy. It involves analysis of society and its dynamics as a result of evolutionary stages of change in the social structure, relative to the mode of production and its consequences on the social relations, which for one largely constitutes Marxist theory of social history. These are found in Marxian interpretation of social evolution from primitive/communal conditions to slavery and feudalism to capitalism, each stage constituting a social formation at large. In recent studies, Amin explains social formation in terms of primitive/communal role, tribute paying mode (as internal conditions within the community), slave owning mode (also as internal conditions within the community), simple-petty community mode and the capitalistic mode of production (Amin, S.1976: 13-14).

Social formations are explained as exhibiting a concrete picture of social progression in unilinear terms: "the development of society proceeds through the consecutive replacement, according to definite laws, of one socio-economic formation by another" (Keiusinen, Q. 1961:153).In this process, as is given to understand, any given social formation qualifies as a definite society being productively active in a definite way to enable itself to enter into definite social and political relations (Marx and Engels, 1846: 1316). However, it is pointed out that the concretization of social formation may not necessarily follow the lines or stages of progression according to definite laws as stated earlier, but merely a succession from one to another, as a matter of historical change. "The general theory of historical materialism requires only that there should be a succession of modes of production, though not necessarily any particular mode and perhaps not in any particular pre-determined order" ("Hobsbawm, E.1964:19). Simpler still, social formation is further explained as a stage of reproduction from one to another (Godelier,M.1976:63-66).

By the above, social formation concretizes and exhibits the condition of society read in the state of its institutions and based on the state of its economy at large in one stage or the other. In Marxian terms, we understand this as the superstructure (political, social, cultural institutions) and the infrastructure (relations and mode of production). It presupposes that the total social structure is shaped purely on economic interests, proved to be a narrow view of social progression, largely spelt out by the economic determinists.

Contrary to it and later much validated even by Marx himself and other non- Marxian thinkers, the facts of a social philosophy or ideology (ideas and action in application), provide the actual and final social force as to the real condition of the social formation. Ideology ensures the relative determinism between the infrastructure and the superstructure and culminates in the total collective formation. Ideology in essence is the prime motive of the condition of the infra and superstructure of any given social formation (Sherman, P.& Wood, James L. 1982:234-235).

Underlying the social formations and with reference to the economic base as a prime unit is the factor of ecology and its use, explained as a dynamic core (Freidman, J.1975:162-163). It implies a double facet of ecological conditioning of the society and social adaptation and there of its form to the conditions of the ecology. Examples are numerous. The study of the Kachins and of their swidden agriculture, conditional to the ecology explains for their *gumsa* (Heirarchial-inequality) and *gumlao* (Horizontal-egalitarian) types of social structure (Leach, E.R. 1964).

Another instance is that of the Mbuti (of African Congo), forest dwellers with hunting and gathering as their economic forte, explaining for their largely egalitarian social organization(Godelier, M. 1977: 9).

In the present study we have identified the traditional period of social formation among the Nagas as rural and agricultural with reference to ecology. Further, economy and society of this traditional social formation is identified with the communal, tribute paying and slave owning mode. As a case of reproduction, contemporary Naga society is identified as less agricultural and less rural than the conceptionally conceived traditional one. This is in consideration of the diversified production activities of a larger cash economy (as against barter) and the role of urbanization, differing much from the traditional village community set up. The contemporary social formation may be identified as equating with the capitalistic mode, more so as a peripheral entity to the capitalistic core of the larger Indian society. The study of social formation further requires the identification of the social groups in focus, considered in terms of (a) Ethnic groups, and (b) Nations (Amin, S.1976:27). In our study, the identification of the Naga society as an ethnic group provides qualification, condsidering the common ecological-geographical habitat and cultural homogeneity of the various tribal groups constituting it. Further as a unit of the diverse collectivity of communities constituting the larger Indian social system, Naga society finds further qualification in identifying it as an ethnic group or a constellation of tribes with a claimed common identity.

Pertinent to the analysis of social formation is that of the emergent social class among the Nagas. This phenomenon concretizes the structutal relationship of the institutions and the economic base of the society (Amin,S.1980:2). The emergence of social classes is explained in relation to the circulation and the control of surplus within the formation. Further, Amin exemplifies the matter with state-class and peasants in the tributary mode, slaves and owners in the slave owning mode, lords and the serfs in the feudal period and in the capitalist mode, the workers and the non workers (1977:23).

In the emergence of the social class phenomenon, the appearance of state control either in the form of a despotic or benign rule is identified as the determinant motive. State control implies a form of rule and organization of a given social formation. It also implies the control and regulation of social production of economic assets, either through exploitation or domination, creating imbalances within (Godelier,M. 1977:9). Social inequality as a result is generated, the unequal nature in terms of control, concretizing the form of the social groups as classes within the formation. Ultimately, it is the social class phenomenon which highlights the analysis of social formation as the main point of issue (Amin,S.1980:24-25). For if a social formation presents the description of a society and its condition as the result of a reproductive stage, social class assumes the priority as the totalising concept. It is explained as where all the social, economic, political and ideological aspects intersect (Terray,E. 1975:86). In other words, class is a collective consequence of the respective institutions that constitutes the social formation. All that characterizes a social formation is concentrated in class. It is, therefore, put into application that the study of a social formation is the study of the class situation within and vice-versa.

Our study of contemporary Naga social formation is addressed to the analysis of the emerging class and elite characteristics as a result of social transformation. In the process, the study uncovers the political and economic changes undergone till the contemporary situation as intrinsic features of the social formation. Simultaneously, the political aspect also explains Naga ethnic expression relative to the identification of the social group to the social formation. The study, as a whole, also implies the aspects of social development in respect of the social transformation it has undergone historically. It implies in abstract, a question of decay, considering its peripheral nature, in relation to the larger Indian social system. This explaination gains clarity in the light of the dependent nature of the Naga society to the productive factors of the Indian nation at large which have aggravated its inability to be self generative or reliant and a viable entity in itself within the larger Indian system.

Class Framework

The study of class in sociology constitutes a major significance. In the identification of the classical school, Karl Marx and Max Weber assume prominence (Heller, Celia S.1969:9). To Marx, class phenomenon is a result of the role and position of men in the production scheme of society and the relationship thereof between the owners and non-owners of capital. By the production scheme or mode of production, he identifies agriculture, industry etc.,and by the relationship of production, the relation between the workers and non-workers of the means of production. The main issue for Marx is the economic situation, where the workers are exploited by profit maximization on the part of the owners of the means of production, i.e. the capitalists.

This finally leads to (i) class consciousness, (ii) class solidarity and, (iii) class conflict (Melvin,Tumin 1978:2). Marx, ultimately concludes that resolution of the given conflict can be affected only when the dictatorship of the proletariats is established.

Max Weber opines of a premise in so far as the economic order (i.e. property) is concerned. He, however, includes power in organized terms of parties to prevail over others and of prestige , in the form of honour to determine status groupings, sharing a common social estimate (Gerth and Mills, 1948: 180-195). He assigned more importance to status groupings as communities although the other factors are not exclusive from each other and often are overlapping categories (Heller, Celia,S. 1969: 22).

The functionalist are principally concerned with the maintenance of social intergration and equilibrium, which view society as a system of action. It owes much to Max Weber and Emile Durkhiem, the tradition later maintained by T. Parsons, K. Davis and W. Moore among others. Parsons defined "social class is a number of actions in role enjoying roughly the same prestige and a system of classes in a number of units linked by differential prestige." (Littlejohn, James, 1972:30). This view implicates power, prestige and property as determinants of class (Parsons, T.1975:69-88). Warner and Lunt define class as "two or more orders of people who are believed to be and are accordingly ranked by members of the community in socially superior and inferior positions." (1941:82). Of recent date, this school has been described as trying to justify class and inequality (Goddard, David, 1972: 60-75).

The conflict school of sociology have a deep bearing on the ideas of Karl Marx. Proponents of this school are Ralf Dahrendorf (1954), C.Wright Mills (1967), to name some who conceive of society as a conglomeration of institutions i.e. political, economic, educational, all loosely integrated to each other. They view that the "unequal distribution of property, power and prestige is seen as representing a special privilege enjoyed by an elite, where advantages in these regards make it more difficult for others to enjoy the good things of life." (Tumin, M. Melvin, 1978:1). This factor provides a continuing source of conflict in society. It is now conceived of as being too far-fetched. While the conflict theory is highly relevant and useful in analysing social and political conflicts in capitalist society during a particular period, its utility and relevance elsewhere are much less." (Bottomore, T.B. 1964:195). On this issue, Dahrendorf concludes that the division of society into warring factions in the strict Marxian sense does not exactly describe the European and other situations (1954:227).

Thorstein Veblen forwards the idea that in all societies, relations between classes are not one of conflict, but of imitation and emulation by one or the other (1931: 21). His views are reminiscent of a situation where the decadent rich upper class is already established and where the poor turns to emulate them by amassing wealth. With Ossowski, a dichotomic picture is presented of "the ruler and the ruled", "the rich and the poor", "the labourers and the non-labourers", all of it constituting a picture of exploitation (1963:25-26).

The above discussion on class can be reduced to three major perspectives: (i) the property theory, (ii) the power theory, and (iii) the prestige theory. (Osterberg, Dag.1979:50-

61). The property theory implies a case of ownership and control over the means of production, that either may mean industry, land and production labour. This is not only a modern representation of modern capitalist industrial society, but also the primitive society characterised by the incidence of poverty. The power theory advocates a case of domination over others, which can either be legitimate (Dahrendorf) or non-legitimate (Mills,C.Wright). It can in itself be a source of prestige and an investment to accrue property. The prestige theory envisages that prestige/status is not merely gained but on the basis of certain other factors, particularly of occupation. Here occupation may be understood in terms of power accrual and wealth attainment etc. These three factors are not exclusive of each other and the phenomenon of class is described as predominantly characterised by these elements.

The phenomenon of elitism addresses itself to the pertinent role of reflecting and symbolising the process of class formation. It is evident with the concept of elite being closely and critically linked with that of class, to the extent that the two are applied synonymously, particularly, in that of the upper class. In this, they are referred to as small and cohesive groups and further, as the ruling class (Bottomore, T.B.1971:198). This finds support in contemporary societies with a record of transition from aristocracy to some form of democracy (Cole, D.H. 1955:106). Raymond Aron provides a clear explanation that the relationships between elite and social class are inevitable and, therefore, are used synonymously. C.Wright Mills identifies the power elite, as a result of being in strategic positions of the great American institutions, the very seat they occupy being the emanator of power. He observes that the power elite as a social class, characterised by power, wealth and prestige, is composed of a small cohesive group (1956:5-12).

It is accepted that the elite represents the upper class in

the context of the class structure of capitalistic societies. Illustrations are provided in the case of the British nobility and its transition from ascribed and landed positions to the field of industry, in which they significantly lead. Further, in the United States, the case of the southern landed masters and their transition to the level of 'business aristocrats' of industry, trade and commerce are presented as valid examples (Giddens,Anthony,1973:166-177).

The elite identification further leads to classification of social groups. In the Indian context, traditional elite were founded on the basis of caste dimension, birth being the determinant factor. Later there were the feudal elite comprised of the Rajas, the Maharajas, the Nawabs and Zamindars with wealth, prestige and power at their command. Further, there have been the elites as a result of colonial experience formed on the British education, whose role in the Indian independence movement was decisive. Of modern times, there are the middle and the upper classes of the occupational and functional elites, in the field of politics, administration, industry etc. (Thakur, R.N. 1981:22).

The elite classification are many and widely based on their occupational and functional basis. Thus, Saint Simon (1807) classified them as scientists, economic organizers and cultural/religious leaders. Karl Mannheim, classified them as the organizing and directing elites and diffused and informally organized elites (Mannheim,K.1956:200). In India, the classification is broadly divided into the urban and rural elites that incorporates the bosses of Gram Panchayat, community leaders, faction leaders, caste leaders, priests and members of the block development committee. Concerning the urban elite, it is further broken into the following categories of (i) politics, (ii) administration, (iii) profession and business, (iv) trade unions, (v) cultural activist, and (vi) mass communications.

With the emergenec of elite and class, the Naga society

represents a pertinent case of social inequality, which in the context of social development assumes a significant position, reflective of contemporary social formations, of Nagas currently we assume the division of the total society into a three tier system: lower, middle and the upper, the last operated synonymously with an emergent elite. Into this, we incorporate occupation as the main identifying feature of elite and class. The elements of property, power and prestige as determinants are understood as incorporated in the nature of occupations, particularly of modern societies. Frank Parkins echoes that "the backbone of the class structure... of modern society is the occupational order" (1971:18). Other sources of economic and symbolic advantages (like status, power etc.) are inherent in the occupational order. The essence of Parkin's contribution is that the occupational structure alone determines the fundamentals of the elite and class phenomenon.

The Naga lower class may be identified in consideration of the occupational nature with the rural population comprising 16,00,452 (80%) of the total population of 19,88,636 in 2001. The main occupation of the Nagas is cultivation, described as without significant surplus (Agricultural Report 2001, Kohima). Agricultural cultivation in Nagaland in terms of occupation and income is further reported as the least paying and a poorer sector of economic activities (Statistical Report,1984,Kohima). The rural population and its occupational practice of cultivation is identified further in consideration that within the occupational order, cultivation is the oldest and most widespread. This is in addition to the fact that the rural backdrop is not significantly penetrated by non-agircultural new occupations. Tht other section of the Naga lower class is identified with the agricultural labourers, unskilled labourers etc., who subsist on income earnings from the daily wages. These sections of the lower income bracket in total comprise the bulk of the Naga society.

As against the above, the middle class and the upper class of the Naga society may be identified with the urban population (19.52% Census of India, 2001), concentrated in such towns as Kohima, Mokokchung, Dimapur etc. They are identified so in consideration of their non-agricultural occupations. In the case of the middle class in particular, a brief on its framework would be relevant, considered the most significant besides comprising a bulk of contemporary class studies. By class identification generally, the aspect of power, property and prestige is intrinsically pronounced, more suggestive seemingly of superlative features as with the concept of upper class-elites. Besides, it also carries the marks of classical approach to class studies, which do not exactly fit into contemporary class studies and identification, with the occupational order in current studies.

Marx, by the term 'petty bourgeoisie', is deduced to have meant the middle class as against the grand bourgeoisie on one and the proletariat on the other, reminiscent of a three tier system of class division. This gains clarity with Marx's criticism of Ricardo for having neglected the constantly growing number of the middle class, those who stand between the workmen on the other hand, and the capitalist and the landlord on the other (Marx, Karl, Capital:Theories of Surplus Value. 1962:93). Here the allusion to forms of occupation itself is self-explanatory.

Stanislaw Ossowski is more tangible with his "scheme of gradation" wherein a middle class is identified in relationship to two polar points of social differentation (Ossowski, Stanislaw. 1963:25-26). With C. Wright Mills, we find another attempt in identifying the middle class based on occupations and allied professions, like the white collar employees and the business section (1967: 275-281). Contemporarily, a framework on the middle class that is in vogue is that of Peter Stearn's model (1979: 383-385). He assigns to occupation the first priority, which as a common denominator identified with Frank Parkins. This is followed by the factor of income (as a precursor to wealth, property etc.). This is followed by what is known as the decision making process (identifying with function and its implication of authority in a given occupation or power emanating from it). Lastly, it is followed by commonly shared values (identifying with subjective collection of social groups, described as common with middle class functionaries in the occupational structure).

The above framework qualifies the Indian social situation, on which B.B.Misra has contributed significantly (1961: 1-17). According to him, the Indian middle class in the contemporary context was mainly resultant to the colonial intrusion. Misra further states that modern inequality of class phenomenon is mainly determined by economic factors (income, wealth, property etc.). In short, occupation is the underlying factor. He further emphasizes on the role of English education, implication of western cultural traits and attitudes. Therefore, the case of the Indian middle class involves the factor of educaton leading to the nature of occupation, which proved as a wedge in the tradition oriented caste system. Misra largely identifies the following classes in India:- (1) the commercial middle class, (2) the industrial midle class, (3) the landed middle class, (4) the educated middle class, (5) the educated middle class (the learned professionals). The first and second group refers to occupations, while the third refers to property/wealth. The fourth and fifth refers to the role of education, analogous to the class situation of the nations with colonial experiences such as among the African (Gutkind and Waterman. 1977:226-284), South East Asian (Rhodes,R.I. 1970:91) and Latin American (Frank, Gunder. 1967) countries.

Misra further provides the characteristics of the Indian middle class. Considering that Nagaland is an integral part of the Indian social system with similar historical experiences, these identification marks have pertinent application in the case of the Naga class formation. The middle class consists of:

(i) the body of merchants, agents, proprieters of modern trading firms including active partners at the top, connected with wholesale trading, manufacturing or financial concerns;

(ii) the bulk of salaried executives, such as managers, inspectors, supervisors and technical staff employed in banking, trading and manufacturing owned privately or otherwise;

(iii) the higher salaried officers of a wide group of institutions and societies ranging from the chambers of commerce and other trade associations to political organisations, trade unions, philantropic, cultural and educational bodies;

(iv) the main body of civil servants and other public servants, excepting those at the top beyond the ranks of secretaries to the government and judges of the High Courts, but including those of the other public services such as agriculture and education, public works, transport and communication;

(v) the numbers of the principal organised professions, salaried otherwise such as lawyers or doctors, lecturers and professers, the upper and middle ranges of journalists, musicians and artists, religious preachers and priests;

(vi) the holders of the middle grades of proprietory tenures of land, such as joint and peasant proprieters, rentiers and farmers of revenue, living on increased income or partially personal management, exclusive of the largest and some of the smallest holders of estates;

(vii) the body of well-to-do shopkeepers and hotel keepers including the managers, accountants and other officers employed in joint stock concerns operating in such fields;

(viii) the group of rural enterpreneurs engaged in plantation industry with a number of salaried managerial hands employed on landed estates;

(ix) the main body of full time students engaged in higher education at a university or comparable level;

(x) the main body of clerks, assistants and other non-manual workers below the managerial and the recognised professional levels; and

(xi) the upper range of secondary school teachers and the officers of the local bodies, social and political thinkers.

In the classification of the middle class a similar analogy is provided by D.H.Cole (1955: 94-95). He arrives at and identifies a similar frame as Misra does, though based on the British class system. With the above proposals of Misra and Cole as background reference, the Naga middle class have been identified. The contemporary Naga social transformation is drawn from the point of discrete tribal communities fused into that of a cohesive unit with a distinct identity. It is further identified by the class and the elite characteristics as reflection of the nature of contemporary Naga social formation. On the other hand, it is also reflective of decay, considering the nature of its dependent-parasitic economy and society largely compounded by its peculiar political culture which on one hand serves its inner mechanism of uniting the tribals vis-à-vis the Indian political entity, yet inadequately participative to the national concept.

CHAPTER-II

TRADITIONAL NAGA SOCIETY
(Glimpses of Social Inequality)

The study of traditional Naga society is beset with various hurdles. One of them is the inadequate literature. Well documented records are meagre. Thus it becomes difficult to identify the broad Naga society with its social, demographic and geographical boundary. Consider the very term "Naga". Even its origin is a matter of controversy. This aspect by way of discussion is omitted as it is not pertinent to the frame of discussion here. It is however now a blanket term labelled on some tribal groups inhabiting a geographical tract of hills, more so for administrative convenience of description by the colonial British Raj; beginning from the mid 19th century. Today, the term also emcompasses as matters of identity various tribesmen in Manipur, Arunachal Pradesh, Assam and even in Myanmar which are not included in the study. At that period of time, the major tribal groups described as Naga were the Ao, Angami, Lotha, Sema and Konyaks to name some. Another problem in the study of Naga society is the chronological division and delineation of the traditional from the non-traditional. The term per-se implies many deductions and meanings as opposed to change, modernity etc. However, our efforts at the moment are neither to create the polemics nor to begin a discourse on chronological issues and its division on a time perspective. So we propose to take shelter in Alemchiba's stand of dividing the course of Naga history prior 1878 as traditional and later, as non-traditional (1970: 129).

The study of traditional Naga society implies apart from social, cultural and demographic aspects, an identification of its physical geography. This can be discerned in the area and boundary lines of the then Naga Hills district constituted in 1866, bordering Burma in the East, the Assam plains in the West and to the north, the unadministered area lying below the external boundary of the Naga Hills and the international boundary between Burma and India, and below it, the Tirap Frontier Area, later to be renamed the "Naga Tribal Area" or identified as the "Tuensang Frontier Division" by the Act of 1935, Section 313 (Luthra, P.N. 1974:7). The notable tribal groups then inhabiting the then Naga Hills were Ao, Angami, Lotha, Rengma and Sema.

In this part of the chapter, we incorporate a representative tribal group, namely the Konyaks from the Tuensang Frontier District. For administrative conveniences, the Konyaks were not incorporated into the then Naga Hills District, but they were very much considered another Naga tribal group (Tajenyuba. 1958:93). They were also subject to the policy of non-interference of the British rule as the other Naga tribes. As early as 1838, Mr.Bronson, an American missionary had been in contact with the Konyaks. In later years, it is from Capt. 'Brodie's account that we learn more about this tribe. Still much later, we are provided with well studied records from Fuhrer C. von Haimendorf, on whose works we shall much rely upon regarding the Konyak Nagas. For the record, the tribal groups inhabiting the Tuensang Frontier Division, along with the Konyaks, were Chang, Phom and Sangtam to name a few.

At that early stage, those tribal groups were not without attention for several reasons. This may be observed in the nature of contact, subjugation and eventually administration imposed upon them by the colonial British power. Needless to say, this was met with great resentment and antipathy, even revolt from time to time (Tajenyuba. 1958: 105). A consequence of the foreign presence and rule is the continuing Naga political impasse the Indian government and society has to contend with today. British control led to the fusion of the various tribal groups into that of a united front, under the name, Naga, in opposition to the British rule. In this early phase, lay the seeds of disruption of the nature of the self-contained various Naga tribal groups.[1] They were in course of time transformed into that of an ethnoc minority collectively within the Indian social system, parasitic and non-productive, as shall be evident in later discussions.

In the process of all these time bound transformation, the Ao, Angami, Lotha and Sema Nagas maintained a dominant social role and are even now, better developed than the other fellow Naga tribes, It is because of the early descriptive accounts of these tribes by J.H.Hutton, J.P.Mills, W.C.Smith, M.M.Clark among others, that we are able to glean a modest picture of a collective unity, a single entity of being 'Naga' out of the fusion of these tribal groups in the conceptual frame. It is also found that in later social experience it is these tribal groups that could provide an image, who would later subscribe to the new common identity as one people, namely of being a Naga tribe.

We are also informed that the blanket application of the term Naga on those tribals were also due to reasons of social and cultural affinity, similarity in physical make up and martial prowess on the objective side, coupled with the subjective ties maintained within themselves for primordial reasons through the ages. This gains academic credence by examination of the monographs based on those tribals by the early scholar-administrators and missionaries.

The scanty early accounts are further augmented by

colonial official records like the Foreign Proceedings of the Government of India/National Archives, New Delhi and the Assam Govt. records. Most of these reports are now available in published form and a larger bulk still remains to be published. Some presentations of these published accounts are Elwin's (1944) and Chakravorty's (1938) and later still Tajen Ao's (1958) constituting a meagre amount. It would be safe to surmise that a greater part of the history of the Naga tribes is unaccounted for, most being lost to obscurity in the passage of time. What remains at the best are the oral tradtions. It altogether does not mean that those tribal groups were left in geographical isolation and mental insularity. On the contrary, they had been maintaining trading and feuding contacts with the people of the plains of Assam since the 2nd century A.D. of the Christian era onwards (Alemchiba 1970: 31-6). Also the Ahom Buranjis are a rich source. Tributary relations and reciprocal aid had as it appears, greatly characterised Naga tribal contacts with the Kachari and Ahomiya kingdoms of the Assam plains (Bareh, H.1970: 15-56).

It is, however, contact and encounter with the British power that led to greater sociological consequences of transformation of the tribals. It was in the first British expedition to the Naga Hills in 1832 led by Capt. Jenkins that brought the British into the contact with the Nagas. In this instance, it was with the Angami Nagas. Far from being friendly, it was a disastrous encounter for the Nagas ending in fierce combat, with the tribals taking a beating at the hands of the well armed foreigners (Nagaland Govt. Publications. 1973: 24).

It took the British power ten major expeditions spanning eighteen years to contain the Naga tribals militarily. The tenth expedition was led by Capt. Vincent, which in defeating the Angami tribals in the historic Battle of Khonoma in 1850, marks the advent of British control over those tribals

(Tjenyuba Ao. 1958:40). However, the British did not occupy the hills physically, as the then decision of the Governer General, Lord Dalhousie, was to maintain a passive policy of no-interference in the day to day life of the tribals (Alemchiba, 1970).

In 1866, the British made the hills inhabited by the Angami, Ao, Lotha, Rengma and Sema into the Naga Hills District under the control of a deputy commisionner, based at Sibsagar, Assam. Even at this stage, the British pursued the policy of non-interference or 'mere political control' from afar (Yaden, L.L.1970: 14). However, tribal aggressiveness, occasioned by raids into British administered plans of Assam and Manipur, affected a change in British policy: a proposal for gradual physical occupation of the hills and control of the tribals was formulated (Tajenyuba Ao 1958: 55).

The Lotha tribal area was annexed by the British in 1875. A levy of house-tax was imposed as a payment for the cost of administration in 1877. In the same year, through the permission of the British Secretary of State, London, the policy of physical occupation/control materialized. Accordingly, Kohima (presently the state capital) was occupied in 1878 as the headquarte of the Political Officer of the Naga Hills. In the same year, Wokha in the Lotha area was occupied (Nagaland Govt. Publication, 1973: 6). The Sema tribe and area were brought under control in 1884, marked by the capture of Lungtang village. Again this was followed by the eventual control of the Ao tribe, with an area headquarter established at Mokokchung in 1888 (Tajenyuba Ao. 1958: 74-75).

The records of traditional Naga society are based on accounts made during the British encounter with the tribals and the subsequent period of administrative control. Church reports also have information gathered during proselytisation process into Christianity of the tribals. Such reports were authored by W.C. Smith and M.M. Clarks (1924 & 1978 respectively). The rest may be safely surmised as belonging to the rigours of enterpreting oral traditions, customs and lores, which are slowly fading to obscurity.

With a view to present the traditional Naga society, it is expedient at the outset to arrive at a generalized picture of the various Naga tribes and later, a description of their specific studies. This generalized picture may consist of the aspects of similarity between the various tribes, which may be identified with the following items:

1) Each of the tribes inhabited a respective area in the hilly tracts of the then Naga Hills District.
2) Each tribe was divided into several major clans. Further each clan was composed of several lineages and phratic groups.
3) Each tribe was reportedly endogamic in terms of the union of sexes, though clanwise, exogamic in practice.
4) It was a rural society divided into villages. The village served as a natural unit of organization, self contained and self productive.
5) The villages were further constituted on a composition of several exogamic clans and again physically, divided into localities or *khels* largely, representing a clan, or a group representing various clans, having joined the village in stages.
6) The village society is described as being community oriented, a corporate attitude being greatly manifest in village activities. These factors are believed to be the motive reasons leading to belief of traditional Naga egalitarianism. It is now however realised that community-corporate activity were mainly a convenience in the relations of production, in fact circumstantial owing to the harsh environment.
7) It was an agricultural society with self-sufficiency. The system of production was either settled terrace

cultivation as with the Angamis or shifting cultivation (jhumming) with the other tribes.

8) In the administration of the village, there were variations from tribe to tribe. With the Angami, Ao and Lotha tribes, a form of republican/democratic rule prevailed though with various degrees and with the Sema and Konyak, it was the rule of omnipotent autocratic chiefs.

9) Contrary to popular belief, traditional Naga tribes were not exactly classless. Data show that social stratification and inequality as opposed to egalitarianism was a rampant feature.

10) Relations between the tribes are described as one of love/hate relationship. Literally, it meant a state of neither extended hostility nor enduring friendship. The same could be described of villages. This was a situation greatly characterised by the incidence of head-hunting, valued as a practice of self evaluation and social elavation, the number of heads taken determining the prestige and status of being a warrior. It was also a form of surplus generation, for in such battles, prisoners could be apprehended and made slaves, whose extra labour, as oral tradition informs, enhanced the paddy cultivation, besides accruing social prestige to the individual warrior concerned. Slave ownership served dually, first as a measure of achievement and thus equality for the established warriors and secondly, as point of inequality with the less achieved or non victorious. Internicine raids in other tribal or village lands and loot of booty was another, for creating a grey realtionship. This practice was equally valued, for it reaped equal prestige on the part of the prepetrator.

11) The religion of the tribals are described as animism, which had elaborate rituals, to which many

interpretations were involved and attached. Consequently animism proved to be a source of many social constraints.

The above generalized picture of the various Naga tribes enables us to conceptualise a picture of social formation of the traditional Naga society. However, for a better understanding of traditional Naga society, as earlier stated, a descriptive account of the tribal groups individually becomes expedient for despite the similarities, each group exhibited peculiar differences on its own merit. It was on such differences that the respective tribes maintained their own identity.

The peculiarity, differences and dynamics of each group becomes clear on the analysis of their internal social arrangement of stratification, nature of rule and power system etc. This particular approach will take the village as the natural unit of study for all the tribal groups. In this study, we shall consider the Sema, Konyak, Ao, Angami, Lotha and Sangtam tribals. Data will mainly be drawn from the works of J.P. Mills, J. Hutton, Christoph Von Fuhrer Haimendorf and local oral traditions, and some direct from the field.

About inequality, it is said that aspects like equality in totality or non-dominance by anyone over the other in any form are not imperically encountered in human society (Berreman, Gerald D. 1978). Likewise, of traditional and societies of historical periods, it is equally difficult to come across data of purely egalitarian societies. Thus, even of colonial records do not indicate anything tangible as to support the existence of egalitarianism among the Naga tribal groups that they encountered, who then were, so to speak, in a state of utter undevelopment. Fried (1960) described egalitarianism as unranked organization, in which the division of labour is exclusively based upon sex, age and personal characteristics. Of the Naga tribesmen of pre-colonial times and even under basis of existing traditional practices in contemporary Naga villages, Fried's presentation is difficult to be comfortably interfaced with the entertainment of generous ideas that past Naga tribes were not characteised by inequality. Bohanon (1963) would come closer to providing credence to the validity of the existence of inequality in traditional society in his presentation of "ranked organization" or more precisely, "kin-role ranked system", which closely identifies with that of the Naga tribesmen.

We stand with that claim that traditional Naga society was characterised by social inequality, when placed beside the argument that most tribal communities were riddled by one form or the other with perceived social differences within themselves. Fallers (1973) thus states that when a process of evolution prevails over matters of social differentiation within society, social inequality is a natural consequence. Of the Naga tribesmen, it would naturally have been that dynamics of self and alter evolution and thus creation of a form of inequality peculiar to each tribe was a rampant feature. Thus similarly, Andre Beteille (1980) strongly reflects that differences in society becomes inequalities when scales are applied to it by cultural construction in their given condition. His statement strongly, although maybe not directly in this case, corroborates the case of inequality in traditional Naga society.

The Sema Naga

Considering the village as the basis of Sema society, the internal social organization is described as stratified into: (1) Akekao (the chief), (2) Chochomi (pre-eminent members, advisory council to the chief), (3) Kekomi (the nobles related to the chief), (4) Aluzhi (inter-age group divisions of both sexes of the village), (5) Mughemi (slaves, destitutes, dependent on the chief and his personal guards etc.) *Akekao (the chief).* He is accredited as the founder of the village usually named after him. By tradition, he is the progeny of a chief, who for reasons of being preceded by an elder brother in succession, or the father being still alive or refusing to remain a mere noble, leaves his parental village to found a new one. The chief assumes the supreme position in respect of power, status, wealth and property. This is shared into by the chief's lineage, constituting a class within the clan the chief belongs to. Hutton describes the chief as "the real pivot of the Sema society". The chief is the only decision maker in the village. He formulates the policies in relation to other chiefs and villages, for village administration and legal adjudication, including day to day affairs. Only in certain customs common to all, does the chief assume a modest position of being merely a moderator or observer.

In terms of wealth and properety, by virtue of being the village founder, the chief claims the major portion of the land, the rest being divided among the village citizens, who again will pay the chief a portion of their produce from their land. This assures the chief of being the richest besides being the most powerful.

Even in war, he is the supreme commander who directs, leads and commands. The Sema chief is a conglomerate whole of multiple roles and positions that are ceremonial, social, political and economic akin to Richard Thurnwald's observation of tribal primitive chiefs (1932: 180-81). In the chief, begins the unit of Sema village social organization and stratification.

Chochomi. It is an advisory council to the chief, composed of the clan-wise pre-eminent members in the village, representing the common folks. They are chosen into this position by the dint of their personal merit and experience of customs and social affairs. They advise the chief and are consulted upon in matters of custom and tradition.

Being close to the chief, the Chochomi members also gain certain status and power. They act as the chief's heralds, settles legal matters on his behalf and generally act as his deputies in the village administration. In the Chochomi, a function can be attributed in stregthening the position of the chief by having its members partially share in his powers. It provides a sense of involvement and thus stems jealousies and resentments from various quarters.

Kekomi. This is another stratum in the village social organization consisting of the chief's relatives, both from the maternal and paternal side. They share in name and respect with the chief as being a royal member. Besides it, they are devoid of any power and economically, no better off from the commoners. This of course excludes the chief's lineage in the clan and immediate family members he belongs to.

Aluzhi. They form the major stratum of the village social organization. They are the village commoners of all the clans. Within themselves, they are divided into age groups of both sexes, each group corporatively tilling the lands in turns besides being responsible for all programmes affecting the village, involving group physical labour.

Mughemi. This constitutes a band of people, mostly slaves, social outcasts and destitutes that do not belong to the legitimate village social organization. They are totally responsible to the chief, pledge all loyalty to him and in return are well looked after. They do not have rights or status. They serve the chief as personal soldiers and guards besides being workers. Hutton describes them as 'churl' and alludes similarity to the European feudal system. They are provided land by the chief and a major portion of its products are returned to him.

The Mughemi sharply reflects the social inequality in the Sema village set up. By its peculiar relationship to the chief, the latter's position is distinguished as opposed to the commoners. In fact ,the mughemi resembles the 'margam' (dispossessed,slaves etc.) of the Kachins of highland Burma and their social set up (Leach, E.R. 1964:61-62). It becomes clear that the Sema social organization begins with the chief, despite the village being the basic unit of the society, with social stratification assuming an established feature. Despite similarity with others tribes, this distinct feature within the society as a peculiarity differentiates the Sema tribal group from others.

The Konyak Nagas

Besides sharing similarities with the other tribal groups, they have their own pecularities that distinguishes them out. The tribe is divided into two major groups, on the basis of certain linguistic and institutional basis, the Thendu and the Thenkoh. Similarly like the Sema tribe, Haimendorf says that the Konyak village can be taken as the basic unit of corporate unity though on a larger scale. Each Konyak village is divided into several wards, each ward centred around a morung (male dormitories). Each ward is composed of several exogamous patrilineal clans, which are further composed of lineages. They are all arranged in a manner, horizontally. Cutting across this vertically, each Konyak village has a social division of people into unequal classes. They are the chiefs and the commoners. Between these two polarised groups, there exists an intermediate group, composed of both the aristocrats and commoners, linked by the mechanism of marriage. At this early stage, it may be noted that class divisions and inequality was more rigid and conspicuous among the Thendu group than the Thenkoh.

Konyak Social and Class heirarchy is the following:

Thendu Group			Thenkoh Group		
Ang	=	Chief.	Wangham	=	Great Chief.
Wangsu	=	Intermediate.	Wangsa	=	Lesser Chief.
Ben	=	Commoners	Wangsu	=	Intermediate.
			Wangpeng	=	Commoners.

Their social and class division shares affinity with the 'gumsa' (heirarchical) institution of Kachins of highland Burma. Here, with the chief's clan and lineage at the top, the class division is on the basis of clan heirarchy and also lineage heirarchy within. It assumes the summit in the heirarchy in terms of wealth, property, power, social status and religious position. The eldest member among the various lineages of this clan becomes chief. His selection automatically also raises the position of his lineage within the clan.

The Ang/Wangham (chief)- The Konyak chief is deemed an autocrat, the final and highest embodiment of political, economic and religious authority. In terms of wealth and property, he is the richest man followed in descending order by other lineages and clans of noble descent. For all purpose of policy, rule and administration of the village and other tributaries (provided he has), it is the chief who formulates the policies and decides the issues assisted by a council called "neingbos" who are the morung leaders in each ward. Such is his religious position, no commoner can kill him in war, lest they incur his magical wrath. Commoners cannot look him in the eye for the same reason.

The chief can be overthrown or removed only in one instance; the commitment of incest, which is taboo to all as he is the law maker, the adjudicator and religious head. It is believed that an act of incest will bring doom to the village and its citizens. In such an instance, he is removed, often killed, the act believed to be cleansing of the air he has defiled.

The *Wangsu* of the *Thendu* group and the *Wangsa* and *Wangsu* of the *Thenkoh group* constitutes an intermediate group between the *Ang/Wangham* (chief) and the *Ben/Wangpeng* (commoners). They are the products of hypogamous and hypergamous alliances of the chief's male and female relations with those of commoners marrying into the aristocratic ruling clan. They constitute a second stratum, next to the ruling clan in terms of power, wealth and status.

The basis of the Konyak social organisation, stratification and class division is the clan in village. The other clans composes the other strata of commoners. Added to it, the institution of slavery distinctifies Konyak social inequality . Slaves had no rights whatsoever. They could be possessed by anyone provided he could pay for them or be heroic enough to capture one in battle or in raids. This was the uniqueness of the Konyak tribals, described as a European feudal situation in miniature.

The Ao Naga

As with the other tribes, the village for the Ao tribe is the social, political and economic base. The traditional system of rule and power in an Ao village is vested in the Putu menden (council of elders, literally it would translate as Seat of Generation). This council is generally of the elders of the respective clans in the village and all are generally represented. This council is responsible for the village administration and other matters of importance affecting the whole village community. With most of the clans represented in the council, the system of rule is described as democratic. Every man's voice and grievance is channelled through to the council through their representative.

The Ao tribe by way of language is characterised by two dialects namely Mongsen and Chungli. Each group generally in a village maintains their Putu menden (council of elders), wherein the nomenclature of the functionaries differ on the basis of their dialect.

Mogsen Group. **Putu Menden.**	**Chungli Group.** **Putu Menden.**
1. Tsunger (leader of the council)	Onger (leader of the council)
2. Samen (council member)	Tazung (council member)
3. Tsadangodang (assistants)	Chidangodang (assistants)
4. Yanger lemsa (peer group division)	Zunga lemsa (peer group division).

The Tsunger/Onger and the Samen/Tazung specifically carry the responsibility of village administration, formulation of village policy in relation to other villages and most of all adjudication in matters of dispute and litigation, explained as rampant in the Ao villages. "This arrangement according to Longchar "shares resemblences with the structure of a modern parliament" (1995 Ph.D mss). The Tsadangodang/ Chidangodang as assistants look after the comfort of the councillors in their sessions, such as cooking, running errands and as porters when councillors undertake journeys. The Yanger lemsa i.e. peer group divisions – for an initiate begins from the age of 15 – 16 divided into eight ascending stratums till the age of fifty, considered to be the conclusion of "youth", a concept, that varies from tribe to tribe – society to society. Their life generally begin in the Ariju (youth dormitory/ Morung) that in itself was an institution of passing down knowledge, wisdom and duties to find qualification as a true citizen of the village and tribe. Most of all, they constituted the warrior cohort for village defence.

Members of the council of elders are accorded a special respect, in fact a social status by virtue of their membership, which is largely determined by their personal merit and experience. Their membership also accords them certain special privileges. In all cases of fines exacted, generally domesticated animals like cattle and pigs, it is divided among themselves. Partakings in such divisions of spoils sanctioned by the *village will* entails great social prestige. And a recipient of it receives great social standing. Membership in the council is one *potu* (one generation = about 30 years), provided physical and other inconveniences do not affect the incumbent.

Social inequality was a rampant feature manifest in the fact of slavery among the Ao tribe. Slaves were deemed as property of the master. They had no rights whatsoever and could never possess any property at all. This slave master relationship could be viewed as an economic system, much as Neibor defined the phenomenon (Neibor, H.J. 1960). It is reported that slave owners were economically richer than their neighbours, obviously as a result of the slave's forced labour into their production scheme of paddy cultivation. Besides, slave masters were usually, as oral tradition reports, the noted warriors, who had acquired the slaves in battle and in raids on alien territories.Slaves were also traded and bartered, usually for grain or land.

The institution of slavery clearly indicates Ao tribal stratification and social inequality in the village, much in contrast to popular belief of Naga traditional egalitarianism. This had further social consequences, leading to the formation of village social classes in terms of economic factors. Slaves were a polarised segment of the village society as a dispossesssed lot in the relations of production and an investment in the means of production. Slaves among the Ao tribe, it is said had no personal name and no membership/ representation within a clan. True to their negative social position and to distinctify it, they were always made to eat cold leftover food.

Mill's monograph on the Ao tribe (1920) is replete with mention of rich individuals and families, representing the village economic social class. They were probably those with more granaries than their counterparts, as a result of extra slave labour in their fields or inherited. Then the village society, lacking a monetary system of exchange, paddy grain was operated as measures of wealth and exchange. Members of these social classes accrued their position by hosting feasts of merit to the village folks, added with the sacrifice of *mithuns* (then and even now, a rich man's cattle and a symbol of wealth). Even Mills recounts one Mr. Imnameren of Mokoktsung (presently Mokokchung village), who is reported to have sacrificed 40 mithuns once, in a single day.

Members of this social class were those accredited with hosting feasts of merit, reflected by the placement of "Y" forked wooden posts in their compounds. Most members, as tradition states, born into such families were expected to outdo their forebears. Such perpetuation of social classes could mean on the one side, the perpetuation of inequality in the form of slavery on the other.

Even clans in the vilage were stratified. Clans or a clan, having founded the village, irrespective of their social standing in other villages; would be accorded a certain prestige of being the eldest and, therefore, the corresponding respect and deference. This accordance of prestige would be graded down with other clans having joined the village later, being posited to a lowerscale in the scheme of gradation. This clan gradation within the village also entailed certain norms of behaviour, address and reference.

The Angami Nagas

By all appearances, the village as a frame for the Angami Naga is viewed as the base of social organization. However, this appearance does not advance any further. In fact, the village entity merely serves a political and religious expediency of being a unity in the common face of opposition from other villages and tribes. This is a tenuous arrangement, which in times of internal stress or misunderstanding tends to splinter into respective clan composition and thereof locality organization (Khel). The overall village concept at most times can be reduced to the fact of merely inhabiting a common geographical area physically. As Hutton explains (1920: 109), the real unit of social organization, as is evident in the sociological perspective is the clan, which is so distinct that it gains the appearance of a village within the village, demarcated by stone boundaries and even fortifications.

In terms of government, law and justice, the Angami is described as practising a novel form of democracy, where every man is law unto himself. Capt. Butler reported that "every man follows the dictates of his own will, a form of the purest democracy which is very difficult to conceive of as existing even for a single day; and yet that it does exist here is an undeniable fact" (Journal of Asiatic Society, Pt. 1, No.

IV, 1875). Naturally as a consequence, the oral records are replete with instances of persons, defying established customs and social norms, much at the cost of village social order, particularly between clans, representing different *Khels* of the village. For a semblance of order and governance, the Angami Village maintained a *"pehuma"* (chief), whose authority was nominal, merely reflecting the general will and dictates of the village population. For a chief's appointment, qualifications were mainly on the basis of bravery, martial powers and oratory (Gundevia, Y.D. 1975:25). The position was hereditary and the function, merely to lead warring parties against a common village enemy. Beyond this, the chief enjoyed no extra privileges whatsoever, no authority other than mentioned, except perhaps a slight measure of influence over warrior colleagues to curry favours. As Capt. Butler further reported, the "pehuma" is merely *primus inter pares* and *protem* (JAS, Pt. 1, No.IV, 1875). The seat of the chief could not be perpetuated owing to reported instances of the village being at conflict with another village or tribe and frequently, as a measure of distraction from internal village discords, lead a head hunting or raiding expedition elsewhere. It appears that in the institution of the chief, a measure of tact and diplomacy was implied, for in calling for a martial expedition, the village would unite and a measure of order entailed.

As a practical measure for day to day affairs of general village administration, particularly for adjudication over disputes and offences, an informal *council of village elders,* representing the various *khels* and clans would operate. Their functions as it would appear qualified the concept of a democracy, to the extent that their arbitration carried the general will, particularly that of the representative clans, constituting the village. However, as is understood, in many matters despite the general village administration and that of social ordering, the individual was law unto himself, particularly in those aspects unbridled by custom or convention. This all the more characterised the weak bonds of social relationship of the Angami village. As a matter of fact, even contemporarily, in most Angami villages, "relationships among the clans are not always friendly and quarrels between them often resulted in violent clashes (Ganguly, Milada, 1984:54)".

With the overall Angami tribe, the clans, the family and the individual place large emphasis on their pedigree, involving an ascribed status of being placed higher than the other. This was particularly pertinent in the overall Angami social organization of the traditional fold. Hutton's recorded traditions state that the Angami tribe is described as having descended from two brothers/cousins who came out of the earth. From them arose two social divisions known as Kepezoma/Kepopoma the elder and Kepepfuma/Kepepvuma the younger. These were exogamous social divisions from which all Angami exogamous clans and phratries took descent. Social relations between them were characterised by strict adherence to certain norms and conventions- to the extent that on public and ceremonial occasions, the members claiming descent from the Kepezoma/ Kepepoma division will eat, drink, speak or address first or initiate any matter to be followed by the members of the descendants of the Kepefuma/Kepevuma. Rooted in such traditions, despite Angami democratic attitude of the individual being master unto himself and equal as any, there were traditionally an established form of social stratification.

Further, the major divisions of Kepezuma and Kepefuma had a direct bearing on village social formations based on their supposed pedigree. Consequently, among the Angami tribe even contemporarily, Khonoma and its tributary villages, descended from the Kepezuma division constitutes a social grouping considered *par excellence* as Hutton had with clarity pointed out. Other villages and its tributary counterparts were considered a shade lower than that of the Khonoma group, having roots of descent more from the Kepefuma division. This traditionally constitutes a form of enshrined social stratification in terms of status and privileges, even to the extent of belief of natural attributes of persons, although not so extreme a degree of inequality, other than the matter of slavery.

The incidence of slavery among the Angami tribe represents a pertinent case of social inequality of masters and subjects. Slaves had their root in the matter of being prisoners of war, victims of kidnap and of circumstances of dispossession and destitution and thus, reduced to that down trodden position. As with other Naga tribes, slaves among the Angami had no rights or privileges; carried a high economic value worth several cows or other items of equal value as Capt. Butler states. Slaves contributed labour to the masters' fields, thus ensuring higher return in harvest. Besides, they also enhanced the master's prestige and status. Conditions for the slave were harsh and benign, depending on the character and magnanimity of the master. If the killing of slaves for sacrificial purposes were extreme, on the other hand, the adoption of slaves by barren families with rights to inheritance and implicated to the status of free and equal citizens marked the precarious conditions of slaves.

The Sangtam Naga

As with other Naga tribes, the village form the basic unit of social organization for the Sangtam tribe. Tradition states that generally in founding a village, the Singkongwi (the bachelor's hall and dormitory) would be first constructed on priority, only after which the formation of Yangpumji (village council) would be discussed within. Here we understand the role of unmarried male youth, who generally in all Naga villages of the past constituted the warrior force for war and thus in this case, priority to maintainance of village defence posture.

The Yangpumji (village council) is constituted by the Lakhimru (council of elders), representing each clan and locality of the village, where one discerns a form of democracy in so far as representation is concerned. The Lakhimru (councillors) in formal meeting of the Yangpumji (village council) are presided over by the eldest member among them. All the councillors share equal rank and prestige and are assigned respective functions in the village administration.

Another institution in a Sangtam village is the Shang (peer group divisions) in which every male youth on passage from childhood must involve and qualify through the various stages. The life of the Shang always revolved around the Singkongwi (bachelor's hall and dormitory) which had the function of an academy of teaching the culture and tradition of the tribe and village, the arts and craft and warriorship. The Shang also served as free cultivation labour gangs, finding similarity with the Sema tribal Aluzhi, as pointed out by Hutton (1968, Rept. :153). Any Sangtam male in his village, not having qualified the various stages of the rights of passage as prescribed by the Shang would have zero status and never ever become a Lakhimru in the Yangpumji.

In the case of any Sangtam village, its potentialities to sustain itself were dependent upon the dynamism of the Shang and as a result, generating the active posture of the Singkongwi. This is true with other Naga tribes with their corresponding institutions which have been amply observed by Mills that "decaying morungs (bachelor halls/dormitories) meant decaying villages" (1982. Rept :49)

The Sangtam tribesmen in the villages were characterised by a form of social inequality. For instance to become a Lakhimru (councillor) of the Yangpumji (village council), a candidate requires the pedigree of being a member of the founding clans of the village. In addition, background from a family of affluence with records of having hosted a feast of merit were other requirements which according to Longchar is even now the rule in the villages (1996. Ph.D .mss). The above as seen against the incidence of slavery within themselves, traditional Sangtam tribe falls within the ambit of being characterised by un-equal social relationships. Slaves it is said were primarily those captured in raids from other tribes and villages. Often it would be the case as reported that those falling into destitution with no kith and kin to look forward to – eventually would be entrapped by the wealthy and powerful into that subservient situation. If any membership in the Yangpumji is a reflection of inequality in relation to the general public for the Sangtam tribe, on the other in the case of the Ashi Mukhulong (general village citizen's forum), an institution that meets every three years in conference, which assumes the example of a form of inner democracy. It is a gathering, where any village citizen can ventilate their feelings without fear of reprisals, long as it pertains to truth and fact and opinions that constitutes critiques for change, amendment and enforcement (Ibid). And every three years, barring unforseen factors to postpone or defer, the Sangtam tribesmen in their respective villages finds continuity as a tribal entity.

The Lotha Naga

Traditionally, every Lotha village carry the view of being an independent unit. This as with other Naga tribal villages echoes a similar visage of certain uniformities in the Naga tribal existence of socio-cultural stream. It is a depiction that as with the Ao, Sema and the Sangtam, the village by its own merit and achievement found qualification as a self sustaining social entity, within the panobly of fellow tribesmen of other villages.

Lotha villages were generally ruled by a chief and assisted by the Tongti (council of elders). The chieftainship was hereditary, although it did not necessarily pass from father to son, meaning it could have been rotated by succession within the same lineage of the chief (Mills, Rept: 1980). Today, this is felt to have resemblences to that of a monarchy although not in exactitude but nevertheless a nascent form of inequality in terms of authority.

The power structure beginning from the chief and assisted by the Tongti in the traditional frame in most cases, is surmised to have been exercised by the Tongti (council of elders) who represented the respective clans and village localities, in proportion to village population (Longchar, 1996 Ph.D mss). The Tongti (council of elders) were assisted by a lower stratum called Chochang, who are described as younger to the Tongti.

The above descending order of authority tapered down to the Pangki (general village citizens). Within this stratum is an institution called the Yangten (peer group divisions) who are divided into four divisions from as early as twelve years to forty and plus years. These divisions apply to both boys and girls, who in necessity, can be relied upon as labour in the rice fields or any work requiring extra help.

The traditional ranking order as seen above in matters of authority, which also implied relative status and prestige and thereof rewards does not require any hair splitting exercise to be understood as a matter of inequality installed. The other aspect in the same frame is that those clans or families, not involved originally in the founding of the village, despite being accorded most rights and obligations to land and resources as with any other in the village, nevertheless are mentally singled out in the process of social action dynamics – finding translation as not equal with others in the village (Longchar, 1996 Ph.D mss).

With the foregoing discussion, we are provided with a descriptive account of traditional Naga society as a stage of social formation, deduced from the common features they shared at large and also from their respective tribal characteristics, based in the village as the focal point. With the Konyak and Sema Naga tribes, it was a social formation revolving around overbearing chiefs and clans as a distinguished social refernce group, monopolising all aspects of political and economic power. With the Ao, Angami, Sangtam and Lotha Naga tribes, it appears to have been more democratic as compared with the other two, with substantial individual freedom and possessions of property based on personal labour and merit, within a collective community organization. However, social inequality was a rampant feature, with the aspect of slavery as an economic dimension, characterising thr rise of families and individuals to unequal positions and status. With these features of traditional society, its identification as a stage of social formation gains clarity in comparison with the contemporary formation.

CHAPTER-III

COLONIAL CONTROL AND THE NAGAS

The early Naga tribes under colonial control underwent a phase of development in the nature of social transformations, hitherto non-existent within their internal structure. This transformation occurred as a result of several exogenous forces. Here it would also be pertinent and clarifying to embark on a discussion on the nature of tribal transformation of greater India in general, before we actually focus our attention on the process and nature of Naga tribal transformation. It would appear that the course of Indian history is replete with transformation of tribals to a social phenomenon of caste characteristics through contact with the Hindu culture (Kosambi, D.D.1975:27). In fact, the total experience of tribal encounter with the Hindu culture in most cases have ultimately led to the Hinduisation of that tribal group (Srinivas, M.N. 1972:46). For these reasons, it is the popular acceptance with social scientists yhat the 'encounter', irrespective of its nature and reason becomes 'instrumental' for tribal social change that eventually shatters the geographical, social and cultural insulation of tribals in larger India.

The case and nature on Indian tribal transformation is also observed as a process of change from 'tribe' to 'jati' characteristics (Mandelbaum, David.1970:573-619). This view of course is opined to be acceptable only as long as it is confined to the tribal groups of larger India. In this aspect, Bailey's explanation of tribal social change is viewed with considerable qualification (1958). In the case of the early Naga tribals, despite contact with the Hindu non-tribal society of ancient Assam, Naga tribal transformation failed to occur, much less being Hinduized and integrated to the larger community. This becomes evident in examination of the historical relationship of the Naga tribes with the people of Assam as early as 1228 A.D (Alemchiba, M.1970:29). At the most, a form of tributary relationship is recorded to have been in practice which is further evinced to have been mainly cursory, depending on the nature and expediency of the actors involved, in terms of economic or social prestige and status. This gains a strong countenance in considering that Assamese Hindu influence on the Naga tribals were not sociologically incisive or instrumental for any major social impact.

Therefore, it is argued that the nature of tribal transformation of greater India does not exactly fit into the case of the Nagas. Coupled with oral traditions, even recorded history does not provide qualifying information of the pull and fusion of the Naga tribes into that of the orbit of early Indian mainstream, much less, that of the major tribals of the region. Basing on these simple and inadequately articulated arguments, it may be to a larger degree, operated that the larger Indian social milieu did not play a major role in the transformation of the early Naga tribals.

It is generally described that the study of general social development in India has mainly been in the broad framework of the caste system, particularised in terms of caste and occupational mobility, inclusive of the tribal societies pulled into that dimension (Kupuswamy, 1970). These studies also imply a factor of class growth as a significant issue in later events of social change.

However, in the case of the early Naga tribals, the caste factors were non-existent. Added to it, despite unqualified claims of egalitarianism, social inequality evidently was an integral feature, although by relative understanding, differing much in comparison with that of the caste system in nature. These considerations brings to a position of academic light that Naga tribal transformation on a major scale can be ascribed to colonial intrusion into the region.

Historically, the Treaty of Yandabao – 1826 saw to the intrusion of (the British) colonial power to the region at large (Gait, E.A. 1967). This was made possible by helping the dwindling fortunes of the Ahomiya kingdom of Assam against Burmese conquest. British colonial involvement was naturally with ulterior motives of economic gains. The treaty, however, did not bring into effect British interest for trade relations with the Burmese Regent. Nonetheless, the colonial presence in the Assam and Manipur plains afforded them a springboard to further their economic interests. As early as that, the Garo Hills was already under economic exploitation, of having their cotton products siphoned off. For credence, "there is much reason to believe that the country (referring to present North-East India) is rich in many natural products. Its cotton trade (for one instance) has always been considerable and the Lieutenant Governor hopes that instead of our having to burn large quantities of cotton in punishment of outrage, as was unhappily necessary in a few instances, we may find here a new source of supply to Manchester... (British Bengal Report, 1872-73)."

As indicated by the above of such vested interests, it was inevitable that the colonial control would eventually extend to the hills from the plains. An instance can be found in the establishment of experimental tea gardens in the Khamti tribal foothills as early as 1832 by the British East India Company (Miri, Sujata.Ed. 1980). Such types of alien presence on tribal lands accrued native resentments, expressed by physical raids of kill and loot. The Naga tribals being no less in such outrageous acts in the view of the British power, the hills and its inhabitants were in time brought under administrative control. It would appear to be clear that from such evaluations, it was imperative to have the hills under colonial control and accordingly exploit them (Panda, C.R. 1978). Similarly, Kohima was made into an administrative headquarter in 1878 of the then loosely administered Naga Hills District in Bengal Presidency. This is generally taken as the formal establishment of British paramountcy over the Naga tribals and their hilly habitat. Here after, Naga social transformation is largely traced. With the establishment of the British paramountcy in the Naga hills, we can trace the manifestation of a new stage of social formation, through the effects of the exogenous forces they represented leading to social transformation.

The Imposition of Administrative Political Control

The imposition of British control over the Nagas had various consequences in the context of social transformation. The Naga village is considered the natural unit of organization in the traditional perspective (Horam, M. 1975). Each village was a political entity of with its own sphere of control and territory, peculiar from another in its own fashion. The British control shattered the village sovereignty and the maintenance of village and tribal seperation. What was earlier village-state republics and on its own merit tribal distinction was brought under the ambit of one political and administrative control.

In the British power, the Naga tribals could identify a common foe and consequently, a common social opinion that would eventually unite the tribal groups as one people. In this process a tribal cohesion, hitherto non-existent gradually developed. Consequently, it meant the traditional village polity lost its old age practice of self-governance as a compact political unit. Its geogarphical barriers and social boundaries were broken. The villages then, representing the various tribal groups were incorporated into a new political order as unit of a larger system, namely that of British India.

It is noteworthy that the British, pursuing their *'policy of non-interference';* although exerting their supremacy, did not tamper with local customary practice and power arrangements. This particular aspect is described as amounting to a situation of non-surrender of their sovereignity on the part of the Naga tribals, unlike the Khasis, Jaintias and the Singphos (Rao, V. 1976-315). Such an act was fraught with many implications. It gave the Naga tribals room to freely rally themselves and nurture their resentment of the alien rule.

In an assesment, the British rule in reaction made the Nagas conscious of each other, inunciated by their common plight. As such, "the Nagas became concious of the changes and rose to the occasion. They realised that their interest and outlook should go beyond the limits of the village" (Alemchiba, M. 1970: 162). As a result within the new situation, the Naga tribes could transcend their age old tribal and village differences and insulation. In their common resentment of the colonial rule, gradually grew political aspirations for solidarity.

It is opined that in the early Naga tribal fusion consequent to British control, was manifest a process of nation making resultant to the common goal of political solidarity. This gains credence in the explanation that the emergence of a united machinery (i.e. awareness) for self-generation and control weilds and decides the fate of the various members, much led by a social class in persuance of the collective goal (Amin, Samir. 1976:27). Here is discerned a case of political cohesion as an element of social transformation on the part of the Naga tribals. It can be identified in the eventual emergence of the "Naga Club")in 1918, reflecting Naga resentment to alien rule and thereof political aspirations for self determination. (Yonuo, Asoso. 1974).

In the Naga Club, many translations can futher be drawn. It not only represented a transformation and there of development of tribal groups with a wider political outlook, but also within it arose a section of people, who apart from the collectivity, could exploit the fluid situation for the promotion of political aspirations not possible earlier, in the custom ordered village polity. With the emergence of this set of power oriented people, another phase of development occurred in Naga history, which could affect and have a significant bearing on contemporary situation, in the shape of the Naga political impasse as well in the nature of the state formation as a unit of the Indian federation.

Christian Proselytization

It would appear that the Naga tribal religion greatly determined the ethos of the people. It is believed that it functioned to the extent of controlling the behaviour of the individual life and that of the village society at large. It is explained as involving many elaborate rituals and ceremonies strengthening the belief of the people and thereof the social bond of the total society of the village. Animism, as it were, at that time served the people well (Miri, Sujata.Ed. 1980: 84).

Introduction of Christianity into the region had colonial historical antecedents. It first appeared in 1836 at Sadiya-Assam on the invitation of the colonial power, led by Reverend Nathan Brown and O.T Cutter. As earlier explained, they were called in with the hope that Christian teachings may pacify the hostile Khamti tribals, whose bellicosity was hampering the tea project of the East Indian company, one of their political economic pursuit (Miri, Sujata. Ed. 1980: 87).

Therefore in the light of the colonial interests and relative administrative control, as opposed to the aggressive tribal reaction, it may be described that it was inevitable that Christianity would eventually cover the Naga hills. Subsequently in 1872, Rev. Clark entered the Ao-Naga tribal hills;Rev. C.D. King the Angami hills in 1879 and Rev. D.E. Witter the Lotha hills in 1885. In this way, according to colonial policy, Christianity was introduced and allowed to spread, to soften the aggressive nature of the Naga tribals particularly directed to the foreigners and conveniently, bring them under British control (Alemchiba, M. 1975:53).

The number of Christian converts grew slowly in the Naga hills as provided in the

following reports:

Year	Total Population	Christian Converts	Census of India		
1881	94,380	3	"	"	"
1891	122,867	231	"	"	"
1901	102,402	601	"	"	"
1911	149,623	3,308	"	"	"
1921	160,960	8,734	"	"	"
1931	178,844	22,908	"	"	"
1941	189,641	34,000	"	"	"
1951	205,950	93,423	"	"	"
1961	369,200	195,588	"	"	"
1971	516,449	344,798	"	"	"
1981	774,930	621,571	"	"	"

Statistical Handbook, Nagaland, 1973 Census of India.

The spread and the growth of Christianity was slow and only after the 2nd World War, did greater conversions begin. Christianity as a case of transformation and development had various consequences. Much as Christianity as a force had many positive aspects, for instance, the control of head hunting and tribal village wars (coupled with administrative control), it had many unproductive sides as well. Traditional tribal social aspects of corporation and cohesion in the villages and within the respective tribe was largely based on the rituals of their age old religion.

Again, most social practices and customs in as much secular, were based largely on religious beliefs and rituals. It is described as having demoralised Naga communal life (Elwin, Verrier. 1944:14).

Since Christianity remained to be a force in total opposition to what their old religion and practices stood for, many an element of the cultural institution of the tribals gradually faded away. This contemporarily explains for the internal dilemma of cultural expression of projecting themselves as a people, considered that cultural elements by perpetuation and practice provides a sense of identity to the people.

In another dimension, the fact of sharing an organized religion on a larger scale in Christianity provided a basis for Naga tribal unity. Much as Christianity disrupted communal corporate structure based on the old religion, it on the other hand, ushered in a social cohesion. This consequently magnified the awareness of social differentiation between the hill tribals and the people of the plains, who were mainly Hindus and Muslims (Yonuo, Asoso. 1974:53). This may largely explain contemporary social tension and the often expressed inability to properly relate of the Naga tribals to the people of India as a nation and a social system.

Introduction of Formal Education

The spread of education among the Naga tribals is seen in conjunction with spread of Christianity. Just as churches were being established, the teachings of the Bible were translated into various tribal dialects in the Roman script. In the growth of the Christian church was rooted the spread of formal education (Yonuo, A. 1974:119). It is historically evident that formal education coupled with Christianity preceded the actual and formal takeover of the hills by the British. The spread of education meant more for Naga tribal transformation and it was a development, that would greatly replace the very mental frame and idea of the reality of the traditional world.

Prior to colonial entry the Nagas did not possess any form of educational institution, a common lingua franca or a script. The *'morung'* may be identified as resembling a formal educational institution where the boys of the village learnt the lore, tradition and custom of the people, religious practices, martial prowess and discipline. It is now accepted in function as the equivilant of a school (Peseyie, Kevinuno. 1974:15-16). It therefore appears that traditional education was something like a broad process of socialization in the indigenous traditions through what the morung (youth dormitories) imparted to the youth. It is expressed that the *'morung'* ultimately promoted the maintenance of social cohesion and group solidarity within the village (Moasosang, P. 1974:39-40).

The first primary school was established at Molungyimsen village in 1878 (Ghosh, B.B. 1978:263). Most of the early schools were in the primary level and by 1904, there was one secondary, twenty two primary and two soecial schools in the Naga hills district. The number of pupils under instruction in progression were as follows:

1) 1890 – 1891 = 297 pupils
2) 1900 – 1901 = 319 pupils
3) 1903 – 1904 = 647 pupils (Yonuo, A. 1974; 110).

In time, the first graduates were Mr. Kevichusa (1923) and Mr. Mayangnokcha (1926), an Angami and Ao tribal respectively. With the availability of the educated Nagas, a silent movement began which could make possible the generation of new occupations hitherto non-existent, a far cry from the traditionally sole occupation of cultivation. In it was manifest a value for education as a means of social and economic ascent (Kevinuno, P. 1974:17). It implied a sense of reward in terms of status and other benefits, particularly a salaried a profession opposed to traditional occupation (Moasosang, P. 1974:41). It proved to be new avenues for any aspirant for a new life, free from the prohibitions and limitations of tradition and custom. It is popularly described as an entrance to altogether a 'brave new world', where survival would be based on the elements of education.

Currently, feelings are abound that modern education has wrought much to erase community corporativeness and social cohesion as taught in the old 'morungs' of the village society. It is quite evident considering that the education imparted to the Nagas was of western origin. It proved to be latent with elements to foster individual hybridization, coupled with the urban spirit of competition, which opposed the communal corporativeness of the old village society (Bareh, H. 1978:302). Most of all, it were fraught with elements of class development, which is a feature of contemporary Naga society.

The above explanation gains credence in recapitulation with reference to larger India of that early period. It is explained that the policy of the British East India Company have been to educate Indians in the western frame to man their establishments; principally responsible for the emergence of the Indian middle class (Misra, B.B. 1960). Education, then introduced in the hills (though not necessarily to man the company offices) being of the same origin, the genesis of similar class oriented developments are evinced in it, as was with larger India, particularly, from the act of the taking over of the missionary schools by the British Indian government (Alemchiba, M. 1970:157). Then the education as described, was a system more suited for white collar jobs, other than equipping the pupils in the knowledge of their own environment, their own needs and to train them to be better and more useful to their communal life (Moasosang, P. 1974:41). Simply, it is viewed as a case a alienation, a case of radical transformation.

As a case, western education gave the Nagas, hitherto without a common language, a common means of communication, namely the English language (Yonuo, A. 1974:1550). It gave access to absorbtion of many new methods of learning, a sense of unity out of being able to understand each other with a sense of change from tradition. This coupled with their native language also provided a sense of differentiation in which roots of Naga inability to relate to the larger India is evident.

It is to be noted that *Nagamese* (a broken form of the Assamese language), was in usage even before the English language grew as means of communication. Besides even today, the English language is mainly confined to a minority of educated people. Nagamese, as oral tradition states was learnt through trade contact with the people of Assam by the various Naga tribes. It also was taught formally (Assamese proper), for a short period in the early schools too. The fact of different Naga tribal dialects and the absence of a common tribal language made Nagamese the Naga tribals' common means of communication. It is still spoken widely, particularly by the rural population.

J.P. Mills (Man in India. 1948: 45) identified the Naga predicament in terms of their attitude towards education that other than making them fit for ordinary life, an educated Naga expects a ready made government post, described as "a sitting and eating job". Such opinions are self-explanatory of the social consequences and development thereof as a result of western education. Gradually, with the erasure of the community spirit of old, class characteristics and consciousness was a consequence that would polarise the few and gradually growing (urban based) educated section and the rural masses into two major classes. Such factors magnified further with the emergence of new professions related to the process of education, particularly with urban growth. All these processes can be aptly described in a sentence that education proved to be a source of social mobility for the Nagas from their age-old static frame to a new form of social inequality and structure, quite dissimilar to the old form of social inequality.

Monetization of the Economy

The traditional Naga economy is described as of a subsistence nature based on agriculture: existing in a "crude form" (Smith, W.C. 1980). A market is conceived as existing then for the circulation of goods such as food stuffs, potteries, iron implements etc. (Bower, U. 1959:60-2). It is further described as a moneyless economy, though stray incidences of the use of cowry and conch shells are found as a crude form of currency, whose use was never intensive nor extensive and therefore does not qualify as currency in its actual sense and use. The whole market system itself was primitive, compelled more by necessity than by value gains (Bareh, H. 1970:123-4).

It appears that the traditional market in relation to social implications of economic interaction was devoid of motivations for value gains. "A moneyless economy worked well...in which various households depended upon their own efforts to supply their primary needs and the undue ascendency of any particular family or person was automatically barred by the difficulty of amassing wealth, when wealth consisted of in the direct produce of labour in the fields" (Alemchiba, M. 1972:277-78). The nature of these types of evaluations based on single indexes could perhaps have led to contemporary and unqualified claims of traditional Naga egalitarianism.

Another significant factor of colonial control and thereof social transformation as a pertinent case of social development was the monetization of the economy. This is identified by the levy of house tax to defray administrative costs of the area in 1877 (Alemchiba. 1974:205). For the Angami tribe, the tax was Rs. 2 per house per annum, while for the Ao and other tribes, it was Rs.2 and Rs.5 respectively, depending on nature and expenditure of the costs involved (Yonuo, A. 1974:110).

Consequently, "the introduction of a first monetary medium of exchange had tented to alter indigenous standard of wealth and shifted to some extent, the enjoyment of wealth from those with plenty of land and paddy to those in receipt of earning in cash" (Alemchiba, M. 1974:15). It appears that introduction of a cash economy afforded immediate opportunities for individuals to amass personal fortunes and for a few, collect into their hands the means of production (land, labour etc.), formerly accessible to all on communal foundations. This was a development against a moneyless economy in which various households and individuals depended upon their efforts to supply their primary needs (Alemchiba, M. 1974:18).

It would be worthwhile to mention that social inequality in pre-colonial days of the Nagas was an established fact (see Chapter 1), which was in terms of ascribed status for primordial reasons, slavery and wealth, the last composed of land and paddy for those so privileged. This was despite the moneyless character of the economy and the lack of the concept and drive for value gains. However, monetisation as the pre-cursor of a new economy ushered in new social and economic outlooks, radically different from the earlier frame. It set a precedence of viewing economic interactions in terms of value and profit making in a mini scale of capitalism, no different to that of the African colonial experience (Waterman and Gutkind. 1977). It was opposed to an earlier system where relative exchange of goods did not entail relative exchange in terms of number, quality or worth; yet where change of ownership and satisfaction of needs could be achieved.

Monetization as a consequence provided at the greater, an avenue for the common folks to raise themselves up the social ladder of success and to wealth, by mearly earning cash through personal enterprises of selling their labour. It proved a battering ram to shatter the established social stratification of old. They found that they would no longer have to be related solely on to the land and its limited products but also transend their social position by acquiring cash.

In the levy of the house tax, lay the motivation to seek for money in cash. Consequently, the barter system was replaced by the process of cash earning, in the sale of physical labour, on the growing tea gardens and other undertakings in the Assam plains (Alemchiba, M. 1970: 478). Another immediate source of income besides others, was the making of the cart-road communication between Assam, Manipur and the Naga hills and bridle paths within, in which the tribals could labour for money (Yonuo, A. 1974: 110-116). Economic interactions was gradually constituted by the use of cash as a medium of exchange. It altogether proved to be an overwhelming change, because monetization of the economy also meant the growth of new occupations as well. It was the establishment of a new social economy . Inherent in it was the possibility for people to rise in life in a different plane, far from the traditional situation, in fact to a state of social and economic class.

Growth of Rural/Urban Market Centres

It is tenatively accepted that the British intrusion into the Naga hills in the late 19th century first started the process of urban growth. It is also the finding that major urban centres of the sub-continent and that of South-East Asia had its beginning mainly as a result of colonial commercial interests (Broom & Selznik. 1966: 583). Likewise the same analogy in this frame gains application to the growth of urban centres in the Naga Hills.

Contemporary towns of Nagaland grew out of the little villages, which were made the administrative headquaters and posts of the various sub-divisions of the Naga Hills District. Records show that Kohima and Wokha was established in 1878, Mokokchung in 1888 and Wakching in 1913 as administrative posts by physical occupation. Tuensang was established and occupied only in the post independendse period of 1948 to mention a few. However, documented records are non-existent of the nature and rate of their urbanization process. As oral history informs us, Kohima and Mokokchung were in those early days, mainly composed of some buildings housing the resident administrator and the Assam Rifles soldiers deployed for checking the warring tribals. Even till the Indian independence, Kohima and likewise the other towns remained merely a motley of buildings, administrators, clerks and soldiers (Rustomji, N. 1982: 52). The picture was exactly neither rural nor urban in perspective.

The growth of these early urban centres, provided a motley of pull factors, particularly that of activities of a market centre. Such centres provided a focus to congregate in, to expedite and satisfy their economic pursuits and needs, replacing direct village to village and tribe to tribe market activity. Out of such interactions, Naga traders, representing altogether a different profession arose.

By the gradual establishment of communications like cart roads, bridle paths and later proper roads connecting the hills to Manipur and Assam, proved to bring the Nagas and the greater Indian people closer. This helped develop commerce and trade, by which the Naga merchants could have access to the markets of far Calcutta and Rangoon (Yonuo, A. 1974:156). Such factors could help intensify the market syndrome of these early urban centres which would later add to itself greater urban characteristics.

In these early market centres, as oral history tells us, most commercial goods procured and sold by Naga traders to Naga customers consisted of cotton yarn, ready made garments, salt, sugar, food stuffs and canned milk, ornamental effects like brass shells, glass and stone beads and iron wares. This saved the village customers as well as the urban ones from undertaking arduous trips to the Assam plains, besides establishing the structural organization of urban-market syndrome in capitalistic terms as compared to the barter of old. On the other, the Naga traders proved a source to the market in the Assam plains, of raw cotton, bamboo products, pan leaves and medicinal herbs. This in socio-economic terms is identified as the process of manifestation of a stage of social formation under the colonial influence.

Besides market activities, the other factors that those early towns provided was social-contact points for inter village and tribal groups, to diffuse their traditional differences and create a greater sense of awareness of each other as common inhabitants of the same hills. As with the growth of trade and commerce and consequently, Naga traders and businessmen, it also generated other occupations and profession of urban character, greatly related to and determined by the spread of education.

It is to be noted that early urban centres for several decades did not urbanise greatly. It was only in the post independence period with the national policy for tribal development that significant urbanisation and transformation occurred. Greater impetus was added after the grant of statehood to Nagaland in 1963.

The aspects of urbanization as a consequence in the Naga hills , hitherto characterised only by village republics meant a broad division of the society into rural and urban. Urban growth further initiated the process through which the traditional village centred-tribal self-isolation was replaced by a trend of out-migration, resulting in greater social and economic mobility. Urban growth also developed a loose form of social relationship, opposed to traditional village tightknit relationships, altogether constituting a new outlook of individualism infused with education.

It maybe deduced that comtemporary Naga social formations is inescapably linked with the urban growth and the economic implications it entailed. The urban situation represents an environment of relative freedom, as opposed to traditional constraints of customs and practices. It is an arena of freedom and accessibility, where the role of the individual could be greatly stressed and personal enterprise enhanced by the facilities and ideas it provides. It means a detachment from community enterprise and corporated mono-goal activity of the village. It offered altogether a new situation for greater life chances for most directional mobility, with new forms and diversified occupations, determined by personal merit and a measure of education, removed from the ascribed role and place of traditional situation. Further, in the urban growth, was rooted the beginnings of a new phenomenon, namely that of social class characteristics.

The exogenous forces of social transformation introduced by the British control of the Naga tribes is identified as creating a semi-capitalist mode within the society, as early as 1920 (Misra, B.P. 1982:62). This contemporarily have concretized into a real capitalist mode as an extension of the wider Indian social and economic system. We find qualification in the identification of the traditional society as one stage of social formation with its economic, political and social systems peculiar to each of the tribes. However with the British control, it represented altogether a new reproduction of social formation, resulting in a wider collective tribal entity, characterised by non-traditional socio-economic and political aspects. Infact, the British control may safely be described as a point of departure from community oriented-village focalised society of a stage of social formation, to achievement state oriented state of new capitalist dimensions.

As a result of the British control and as characterisive of a new social formation particularly in economic terms, it is reported that money lending with interest accrual was widely prevalent with the Ao tribe. This was a radical development as compared to the traditional period.

Oral history informs that one Mr. Imnameren, made a fortune in this way and was the first to build a building with cut wooden planks and corrugated iron sheets in Mokokchung town, a far cry from the age old houses of bamboo, thatch and reeds. He evidently, was one of many, aspiring for a successful life in a new dimension. Among the Angami tribe, as early as 1921, within the new capitalist formation, prostitution was a regular feature of making an income in Kohima (Misra,B.P. 1982: 54). Such instances, radically departed from the moral values and occupations of yore, reportedly afflicted most of the other tribes too.

Private property in the form of land ownership as oral history informs us became a fashionable feature with the Nagas, a feature that magnified the market situation of the urban centres. It apparently involved the urban settlers engaged in cash earning activities, buying the land from the village land owners of Mokokchung and Kohima, on whose village land the urban centres of the same name were located.This may be deduced as a conditioned deviation due to the influence of the exogenous forces, from community ownership and chieftain controlled landed property to personally achieved private land ownership. The consequence of British rule meant a situation of open chances free from the conventions of tradition, totally representing another stage of social formation.

CHAPTER-IV

INTERNAL ASPECTS OF NAGA SOCIAL TRANSFORMATION

The case of Naga social transformation and later, the understanding of contemporary social formations as a case of development can be drawn as rooted on the consequence of the stamp of colonial rule and later, the effects of union with larger India. Parallel to it, there was also begun an internal process of social transformation, which as a case of development involves a cogent capacity to explain for the nature of contemporary Naga social formations.

We can further understand that the appearance of colonial rule as an exogenous force embodied the elements of political, economic and social consciousness. Accepting these as forces to provide the Naga tribes a certain capacity, the internal social transformation is viewed as "the utilising of resources" to affect favourable changes to transcend the stage of tradition (U.N. Paper, 1969:2). It may also be argued that Naga social transformation as a case of evelopment was not without general awareness and an amount of mobilisation for change. It would also be qualified to say that colonial rule accrued elements of tribal public resentments against it which must have triggered latent feelings for changes like political freedom.

Towns as a Service Network

It is generally accepted that urban growth as is associated in particular with the growth of pre-industrial cities laid the foundation of modern industrial societies (Press & Smith. Ed. 1980:173). It proved to be a change from rural-traditional situation to urban transitional society, oriented on service network and production proliferation. In a similar analogy, the contemporary Naga social situation may be described as largely having begun with the growth of such urban centres as Kohima and Mokokchung and the services they provided.

Besides services, surplus production is generally accepted as instrumental for pre-industrial urban growth (Press & Smith 1980: 149). A similarity can be drawn with Naga urban growth; however; it would be pertinent to state that urban growth in the Naga Hills did not necessarily rely on surplus production as such. It appears that market trade was possible even in the early stages , suggestive of surplus. Yet this appears to have been marginal and therefore not in the level ascribed to urban growth of pre- and industrial cities of other larger societies.

The early towns like Kohima and Mokokchung did in itself, as opposed to the village setting provided many social services that could not be possible or non-existent in the rural environment. These early towns in contrast represented a new way of life, a new type of social organization , a new type of socialization that were beyond the possibilities of the village. It altogether was a point of exposure and thereby, a receptable of forces that would transform the Naga tribals in succeeding span of time. Here , the Naga tribals could avail or be exposed to forces that could help them to transend tradition ascribed positions through new occupations . It proved to be in a significant way, a 'social melting pot' of diverse villages and tribes.

The towns provided the society with a motivation to achieve new objectives hitherto unexperienced, of the reflections of life of what larger India and the world represented for self betterment and consequently, general social social development. Such aspects, as deduced from oral history, motivated rural urban migration , evevtually to prove as a case of social and economic mobility. Most of all, these towns, in the form of administrative centres having already replaced the former village polity, could provide an arena of power politics . In this new power situation, aspiring individuals could by personal efforts prevail over community matters and increase personal influence as an exercise of power. All in all, the towns , by their nature provided service network of new proportions, much to determine internal Naga social transformation.

The case of internal transformation, with the towns as a service network can better be illustrated in the growth of Mokokchung town as a mini example. It actually came into being in 1881 as an outpost. The place, however, was not known by its present name, but by the name of Sangtemla kimong (Sangtemla's site), the name of a spinster who resided there alone, according to tradition. It was in 1888, that the name was changed to Mokokchung and also, made into a sub-division of the of the Naga Hills district by the British India government. It had administrative jurisdiction over the Ao, Sema, Lotha, and the tribes of the Naga Hills Tuensang area, represented by the Chang , Sangtam and the Phom tribes (Sub-Divisional office record, 1889).

Then, the place consisted of the sub-divisional office, his and staff quarters and a contigent of the Assam Rifle sepoys. Along with these, there were the quarters of the *dobashis* (interpreters) giving the place a semblance of a settlement. The *dobashis* each repesented respectively Ao, Sema, Lotha and Chang tribe, acting as a link to their respective tribes by their function for the administration. Mokokchung sub-division was further made into a district in 1957, and in its re-organised form it incorporated the Ao, Sema and Lotha tribes (Deputy commisioner, office record, M.K.G. 1957). It has ever since been divided into three districts in 1972 with the formation of Wokha and Zunhebotu districts for the Lotha and Sema tribes respectively.

Presently, Mokokchung town serves as the district headquaters of the same name. It is located on 25° 13' North latitude and 34° 31' East longitude at a height of 4044 feet above the sea level. It is linked to Kohima via Wokha (state highway 2) which in extension links it to Amguri in Assam. It is linked with Tuensang and Zunhebotu by their respective name roads. It is further linked with Assam by the Changki-Mariani road. The town reportedly possesses a population of 31,925 (2001 Census), which also include defence and security personnel, who actually represent a floating population. The local population reportedly comprises of 24,000 and the remaining 8000, the non-locals (Mokokchung town committee report 2003).

The Town Committee issues the residential licences to the householders , and it indicates 15,558 households, divided into 15 wards with an area of 15.5 Sq.Km. By ward division, the town committee considers Ward 1 to be the posh colony because it incorporates land and houses of the affluent section of the town engaged in trade, business and commerce of the high income bracket. This ward also includes the main government establishments and staff quarters. It forther includes private landed property of those in the higher echelon of the government services. The other wards as per town committee identification are classed as the residential areas of the private and government employed section of the population including commercial areas.

On the main arterial roads are found the main commercial sections of the town joined to the area of the daily bazar. There are a combined number of 958 shops, hotels and other aspects of commerce and business, all large and small. They are largely run by non-locals, although the licence, the building and the lands all belong to the local citizens (Mokokchung Town Committee Report 2003). The body of these local citizens owning houses and lands constitutes the local business, commerce and contractors section of the town. Their holdings in terms of land and houses, constitute the physical structure of the commercial belt as indicated in the belt. Further, this section of the local population is found to be very decisive in the district and and state level politics. As the neo-rich, they control the market situation and greatly determine the state of the town economy in collaboration with non-local businessmen, particularly the *Marwaris*, since they carry a big clout in matters of supply and control of many essential articles and commodities.

Mokokchung town has been aptly described as "service town" (Town Planning Organization, Mokokchung, 1982). The services are identified in terms of administrative, medical, educational and economic-commercial activities. They cater to a rural population of 1,26,449, hailing from 96 villages of the district (2001 census). They further cater to Tuensang, Zunhebotu, Longleng and Wokha districts representing the Chang, Sangtam, Phom, Yimchunger and Sema and Lotha tribes, a total of 7,30,808 population, comprising both the rural and urban, including non-tribals (2001 census). This has been made possible, because Mokokchung is directly linked to these four sister districts as well as it being linked to Assam. By virtue of this, Mokokchung town serves as a conduit to these three districts for most essential services, which in consequence gives more importance to the social role of the town (Town Planning Organization, M.K.G. 2001).

Breakdown of Tribal Communal Spirit

Urban growth, however small and undeveloped in itself, proved to be a great resource in the form of social development. This is observed in the emergence and later, acceptance of the fact of becomimg a more coherent and substantial society on the part of the Nagas by the fusion of the various tribes. This could be largely made possible by the early townships. In this, a pertinent aspect is that of the breakdown of traditional communal spirit of the various tribal groups, through intensified interactions in the urban environment.

The discussion would be clearer by citing the instance of present Mokokchung town, which is basically an Ao-tribe town by its location, although, its growth as a town was not necessarily effected by only the Ao-tribesmen. The characteristics of urban life, as it appears did not manifest itself in the town till late 1920's. Till this period, all that the place could show for itself was that of the administrative services of the sub-divisional officer and that of the law and order maintaining agency of the Assam Rifles, the *dobashis* and a handful of seasonal Ao tribal employees of the government, from the villages.

According to oral history of the town, the first local itenerant settlers were the *'dobashis'*, from as early as 1900, who as the link to their respective tribes were required to reside in the town. They also represented the new occupation as they were paid employees of the administration. They also represented the factor of rural-urban migration. Such persons, that are even now remembered with reverence as the pioneers are (i) *Mr. Imnameren Ao*, (ii) *Mr. Ongli Ngakhu Chang*, (iii) *Mr. Chansimo Lotha*, and (iv) *Mr. Senkalemba*, all deceased. As pioneers of the town, they held a respected place in the memory and history of the town. They also represented a conglomerarion of inter-tribal interaction and co-residence.

Actual urban features developed with the settling of Mr. Noktsura Ao (now deceased), the first to open a shop in 1929, with wide experiences of travel outside the hills as a itenerant merchant. Subsequently, it was followed by Mr. Imlimeren and Mr. Imkongmeren (both deceased), the latter to join politics at a later date as the Vice President of the Naga National Council.

As early as this, it is reported that there were also quite a number of Changs, Lothas, and Semas serving as daily wage labourers, often for the administration and for those local people, who could afford their services.

Other than Mr. Noktsura Ao, there were also other tribesmen who settled down as commercial entrepreneurs providing the town a multi-tribal outlook in common pursiuts. Such persons were Mr. Imlong Chang, Mr. Hopingki Sangtam and Mr. Nivokho Sema who all together, represented the affluent section of the town. With them as the commercial pioneers was begun a phase of rural-urban migration in search of new livelihood and most of all, the beginnings of inter-tribal existence, transcending the communal differences.

A weekly Bazaar was established in 1930. It reportedly covered the villages of the Ao, Sema, Lotha, and Sangtam tribe. Some of these villages are by today's measure, even 65 Km distance long. This enabled villagers to gather and market their produce for cash. It also exposed them to the allure and trappings of the outside world, namely in the form of finished products such as ready made garments, canned foods etc. Such activities in satisfying market needs also helped establish local traders and merchants in an occupation, hitherto not practised through the medium of money. This convergence to the town also fulfilled administrative functions by reversal of places, which earlier, it was the office that had to move out to the villages for contact.

By the above record, we are made to understand that Mokokchung town, basically an Ao tribal town by location, did not necessarily grow to be what it is today on the sole basis of Ao-tribal enterprise. What this pertinently indicates is that the town became a focal point of tribal interaction, which had the consequence of breaking down tribal isolationism and animosity. In this was manifest the motivation for various tribals to view beyond their restricted tribal perspective and arrive at a concept of a larger Naga tribal group. Similarly, to the south of the Naga hills, Kohima town, basically an Angami tribe habitat by location, at the same time, served a parallel function as Mokokchung. Here other tribesman, like the Rengmas, Chakesangs and the Zeliangs could converge and interact. Today, Kohima by virtue of its being the state capital serves as the central symbol of all the Nagas.

By the role and function provided by the early urban centres such as Mokokchung and Kohima in the forging of a common concept of Naga people, led to another social consequence; namely that of the formation of an urban population. This could be made possible by the new opportunities as could be offered by the early urban centres, representing a totally new social dimension, hithterto non-existent in the Naga experience.

The formation of the Naga urban population and its number in particular becomes an arbitrary matter for discussion because of absence of the proper written records. It can be safely surmised that it involved an aspect of rural urban migration, in the quest for new and more productive livelihood. Such a phenomenon on the part of the rural folks would have been natural, with the townships providing a dynamism and a dimension, reflecting the society's inner drive for change. A proper process for urbanization and consequently the growth of urban population is deemed to have had its real beginnings in terms of actual development mainly after Indian independence (Rustomji, N. 1983:50).

We can logically deduce that urban population was very small in number. This gains a credible stand in terms of demographic profile, considering that as late as 1957, the total population of the Naga tribals was only 370,000 (Gundevia, 1975:91). Adding to it that the early urban centres in the actual sense of urbanization were not that evident, the sum of the total urban population would have been minute.

By a tentative evaluation, however minute the urban population; they represented a new social formation in the frame of social development. By virtue of what the towns represented vis-à-vis the tradition-oriented village, migration to constitute the urban population presented avenues for social and economic mobility. As oral history states, the urban environment proved a transition to a better life for the individuals besides contributing to the sense of a larger Naga community.

Shift to New Occupations

The early urban centres proved in itself to be a resource of internal Naga social tranformation. This could be feasible as it proved to be a conduit and a receptor of new social ideas and forces of the outside world, namely that of British India, altogether different and developed in comparison. In facilitating the internal transformation, the new occupations presented a phase of development that would eventually constitute a new social formation.

In terms of occupation, the Naga tribesmen from tradition were in most cases cultivators. It was in economic terms an occupation of mere subsistence. The establishment of urban centres on the other hand, provided in itself a focal point, where new occupations in terms of earning cash could be generated, asides from and also, including cultivation. It meant extra incomes with access to new products availed from the Assam plains of larger India, totally representing a new life style from that of the rural folks.

Oral history informs us that the *tea plantation industry* in the Assam plains were the first to provide a new occupation to the Naga village folks. The villagers sold their physical labour in the tea fields, at first more out of compulsion to pay their house taxes imposed upon them, after monetization of their barter economy by the British administration. Even historical records in this context states of the Eastern Nagas (i.e. the Konyak Nagas) being paid a subsidy of Rs. 200 yearly as early as from 1834 by the British administration. This was owing to a land ownership dispute near Sibsagar and Lakhimpur on which lands tea gardens were established (Michell, St. John. Reprint 1976:211). The versatile use of cash money as it appears, dawned slowly in their consciousness, which later diversified their search for other occupations besides the sale of physical labour.

The new occupations as opposed from cultivation within the Naga society began in the villages other than the urban centres. The first instances of the new occupations were in the position of village pastors cum teachers of the Christian message in rural schools and churches, mostly paid in kind. The first of these pioneers among the Ao tribe of present Mokokchung district were one Mr. Kilep (Pastor) and Miss. Tongbangla (School Teacher) from as early as 1899 (Clark, M.M. 1978:86-144). In them, it could be safely arrived at that early instances of the new occupations were in the form of village teachers and pastors.

Another aspect of new occupations were seasonal trade and commerce on the borders of Assam in terms of cash. Such activities as oral history states were predominant till the conclusion of the 1st World War. It is on record that Naga tribesmen valiantly served in the War Labour Corp and were handsomely paid (Alemchiba, M. 1970:282). Such seasonal, though significant in terms of earning in cash represented new occupations.

It is after the 1st World War that the urban centres in the context of new occupations gained their importance, along with the spread of education. In this aspect, answering for the total Naga society, the Naga Club (1918) is a reflection of the situation. The rationale here is that most members of the club represented different occupations like teachers, pastors, business merchants etc. who were to some extent educated. As pioneers in new occupations, the Naga Club established the first co-operative trading society, reportedly in 1935, which still exists today as the *Ao Co-operative Trading Society* in Mokokchung town (Elwin, V. 1961:49). They, however, in number were not many constituting merely a microcosm of the society.

The urban centres gradually incorporated all the aforementioned occupations into its fold, in the process, becoming itself a conduit for the supply of material goods and ideas to the major population from the outside world and more significantly, enlarging the volume of the new occupations.

As early as 1929, pioneers like Mr. Noktsura Ao, Mr. Imlong Chang, Mr. Hopongki Sangtam, Mr. Imkongmeren Ao and like others appeared as a new breed of men, reflective of change and development and of new social formations of the town. Traders and merchants as they were, their exposure to the environment of outside towns like Tinsukia, Jorhat and Gauhati in Assam were significant to the extent that they would establish a new form of livelihood and social network, not practised earlier. Further they would introduce ideas and tastes that would gradually transform the society at large. Elsewhere, in places like Kohima, similar people were ushering similar forces within. Such people and their placement in the towns established a link between the general society and the outside world. In such a situaiton, the motivation for internal transformation was evident from the exposure to outside ideas and forces .

Early Ao-Naga teachers in Mokokchung were people like *Mr. Mayangnokcha* (the 3rd Naga graduate), *Mr. Kilemsungba*, *Mr. Lolen* to name some. With the benefit of education, the first to enter the clerical services in Mokokchung town was Mr. Anagsoba in the government civil hospital in 1930. With him began a process of educated Nagas entering the salaried services, representing a new occupation different from cultivation. In the same year, others entering new occupations as only the urban environment could provide were one *Mr. Asemjungba* and *Mr.Rendimeren,* employed as a peon and chowkidar in the sud-divisional office. There were reportedly many others, names forgotten, employed as gatherers, sweepers and cleaners of the Assam Rifles. They all represented diversified and a process of new occupations.

As urbanization took place however slowly, the physical structure of Mokokchung also changed, in the form of government approved and designed buildings, even new structures for private households – the ideas imported from Assam. This generated the growth of many local artisans in carpentry, stone masonry, earth cutting, manual repairs and of handling and driving machineries. The names of these local artisans are long forgotten for record. They are however remembered as itenerant workers, moving all over the Naga Hills in search of work opportunities. These skills were as reported orally, learned through apprenticeship in the plains of Assam, following the trade route of the merchants. With them are further identified the diversification in range and kind of the shift to new occupations.

As early as this in the Naga social experience, signs of capitalistic tendencies were registered as an extension of the larger Indian society. The traders like Noktsura Ao, Nivokho Sema, Imlong Chang, Hopongki Sangtam and Imonungba Aier, introduced the idea of *urban commercialism,* the ideas, as admitted by them, borrowed from Assam. As early settlers in the town, they could accrue much urban lands and also erect houses, from which tenant rent could be realised, by which they could elevate themselves as a social leisure class. They also represented the money lending section with interest accrual. In scrutiny, this bears a close analogy of the development of the leisure class of Mughul India of the 18th century (Chandra, Satish. 1982:155-65). This aspect later on was extended in the Indian colonial experience to pervade the whole society. Such development in the Naga society as a novel feature is identified as an extension of the larger Indian historical features. Today, it is reported that 15% of the population of the town belongs to this category who make their living by rents from the urban properties (Chairman, Mokokchung Town Committee 1983).

The shift to new occupations was not exactly an independent phenomenon. Its consequences constitute Naga social development in general and growth of new social formations in particular. Urbanization, spread of literacy and the proliferation of new occupations took on greater impetus after independence. With the shift to new occupations where the Naga tribals could be gainfully employed, began a process of alienation from the traditional mode of production of cultivation. It would in later consequence answer for contemporary under-production and emergence of a parasitic-dependency syndrome. It was after the achievement of statehood in 1963, that an accelerated pace of new occupations was started by the various government institutions, all salaried and ranked.

Urban Achievement Orientation

It would appear that the early urban centres like Mokokchung and Kohima became the main focal points for the Naga community. In their growth, a representation of Naga social development is perceived as opposed to the rural backdrop, constituting the majority. In the urban population then, notwithstanding its small size, a growth of new social formation could be conceived, removed from the traditional melieu. This is further construed as representing change, considering the new occupations they were engaged in, the basic economic factor being monetised, the factor of education as a leverage and greater, the exposure to and the induction of new ideas from the outside world. It could be arrived at that they represented 'proto-bourgeoisie' as opposed to the rural society; the analogy being drawn from the African experience of the Yorubas in western Nigeria (Ehrensaft, Philip. 1972 Vol.3). As a significant focal point, the urban centres in terms of development constituted a base of rural-urban dichotomy, that would eventually polarise into two major division of classes.

The growth of urban centres and its population is described as a manifestation of diversified social activities, a precursor to class development, particularised by role differentiation (Banton, Michael. 1973:43-76). In the same line, the instance of Mokokchung and Kohima and its population represented a section of society as compared to the village society. The aspect that they were characterised by new occupations conditioned to a different type of organization and activity projects their difference unlike that of the village order. They constituted the manifestation of a new social formation, transcending the village melieu into that of elite and class dimensions, determined by new ideas and economic features and different social organizations.

The Naga village society in terms of social order and occupation could be described as merely ascriptive, determined by established conventions. As opposed to it, the urban population in consideration of the occupation and life style, represented a new society, characterised by achievement orientation. In such a social condition, diversification and differentiation could usher unequal social developments, characteristic of class society, the respective occupations being the determining factor. It was inherent with undercurrents to lead to class development as the occupational order is considered the basis of modern class structure (Parkins, Frank. 1971:18).

In Mokokchung town, the proliferation of the traders and merchants and later, the urban commercial leisure section based on rent income provided in itself a conduit and link between the inner Naga society and the outer world of larger India. Their trade in finished products like clothings, canned foods, tools and implements represented a case of their introduction to the British-Indian capitalistic mode of production. Such aspects besides enhancing the business establishment of these people also ushered in the spirit of competition and of market manipulation, never experienced in the Naga village society. In consequence, it definitelty gave rise to a new life style, diverse tastes and new types of social behaviour, greatly manifesting on the members of the clerical and teaching sections, the rising neo-politicians against the foreign rule besides the business section.

With the establishment of Mokokchung town, the peripheral contacts of the general village society with the Assam plains could be diverted to it more concretely and substantially. It became a replacement of the Assam plains, to provide services to the tribal population more conveniently. It became a symbol of the outside world to the rural backdrop, only more closer and accessible to avail services more equitably.

Mokokchung, besides being an administrative and an educational source, also became a service-commercial town. This was a natural development, acting as a conduit of the Assam plains for a source and general market of the Naga consumers.

Mokokchung town as a result, became a focal point of the community, a representation of change and development. It presented a new world, where the aspiring individuals by dint of merit and labour, aided by education, could develop in a manner, like that of the outside world. It meant a social situation unlike that of the village world, where one could be born into an ascribed role and the monotonous occupation of cultivation. It meant a point of transition from tradition and conservatism to modernism and liberalism. It further meant a departure from languid existence to progressive development, characteristic of achievement orientation.

Urban Centres as Arena of more Sophisticated Politics

It is noted that the imposition of British administration in the Naga hills divested the age old self governance of the villages into that of the hands of the new power. It in consequence established a network of administrative links between the villages and the seat of power. As such ever since Mokokchung was made into a sub-division of the Naga Hills District, the villages under its division were linked to it, through the function of the *gaunboras* (village elders), appointed by the government as its agents for village affairs.

It can be observed as a case of re-ordering of the power structure, with the villages shorn of their traditional self-governance into that of a centralised form. It consequently made Mokokchung into a centre of power and administration. By virtue of its divisional headquartership, most of the policy decisions, administrative orders emanated from it, just as decisions affecting the whole Naga Hills District emanated from Kohima.

Such re-ordering of the power structure made the urban centres into arenas of political activities, replacing the village polity. This factor can be identified with the rise of the *dobashi* (meaning those who knew or interpreted two languages) institution. The role of the *dobashi* as a government agent was mainly to interpret official communications to the subject tribals. Each tribe then (in the Mokokchung sub-division) was represented by a dobashi, comprising the Ao, Sema, Lotha, Chang and Sangtam tribes. Below the *dobashis* were the *gaunboras,* forming a chain of command for implementation and execution of official orders. Thus a heirarchy was established with the sub-divisional officer at the top, the *dobashi* in the middle and the *gaunboras* at the bottom. By virtue of being placed at the town near the seat of power, the *dobashi* became more prominent figures than the *gaunbora,* even in the latters's own domain of jurisdiction – the village.

By virtue of their duty, the dobashis were required to reside in the area of the sub-divisional establishment. This answers for the presence of a number of other tribal people besides the Ao tribe in Mokokchung town, as a result of retinues and relatives following the *dobashi* concerned. For reasons of proximity to the seat of power, the *dobashi* also gained an element of respect and importance from the villagers, who could always count on him for privileges and favours. Aside from being paid monthly, they also functioned as revenue collectors, from which they received a commission of 12 ½ %. The *dobashis* by their role and function entailed many other benefits and advantages, which explains for the measure of affluence and prestige of their progenies, even contemporarily. In fact, the *dobashi* institution became a focal point of individual, village and tribal power assertion.

The qualification for a *dobashi* was the knowledge of an extra language, usually Assamese or Hindi then, and the endorsement of the village and tribe concerned, which naturally generated intense canvassing and pooling of resources for the aspirant. Such local level politicking was intensified by the selection of a head *dobashi* from among the representative body of *dobashis*. In consequence, the post of the head-*dobashi* became a covetous one, involving much in alligning tribal forces and politicking among themselves. By local observation, the position of the head *dobashi* represented a picture of the general next to the king.

The *dobashi* institution made urban centres like Mokokchung into arena of power aggregation and the process of politicking. The achievement of being a *dobashi* and still further, the head *dobashi* proved in itself to be a transcendence of the village polity, where one could achieve and exercise power by the dint of personal merit. It proved to be an arena where an aspiring individual could mobilise resources for self betterment in terms of power, prestige and even wealth.

The emergence of urban centres like Mokokchung in to arenas of wider politics effecting all the tribals is evident rom the rise of the dobashi institution. This institution as a focus of local level politics, for so long an archetype of tribal level politics was gradually overshadowed when the hills was made into the state of Nagaland in 1963. The emergence of party politics with wider issues and the election system, coupled with the proliferation of the administrative machine with greater trained and educated perssonell was responsible for divesting it much of its prominence. However, it does not mean it has lost its importance, considering that it has judicial functions based on Naga customary law.

The Assam Secretariat report, Dt 29 Oct 1866, No-4923/ File no-305, referring to the Naga Hills, in a report by J.Geoghegan, Esq; Junior Secretary, Govt of Bengal to the commissioner of Assam, first makes mention of interpreters and Naga assessors in disposing of cases. This is the earliest allusion to the matter of the dobashis and their origin. Thus, after several years of functioning unorganized and in a semi-official capacity, the *dobashi* institution was formally organized and official sanction given to it with certain powers in 1914 in the Naga hills. There after, it gained its actual prominence owing to its autonomous nature of judicial functions based on Naga customary law. After its formal organization, the following personalities to mention some were the coveted head-dobashis in the ambit of the Mokokchung sub-division, reflective of inter-tribal mixture and cohesion (Mokokchung Dobashi Court, 1983). They were:

1) Imnameren Ao 1/6/1914 - 21/10/197.

2) Ongli Ngakhu Chang 28/11/1917 - 6/9/1938.

3) Chansomo Lotha	7/9/1938	-	1/7/1943.
4) Senkalaba Ao	1/7/1943	-	30/11/1960.
5) I. Kawato Sema	1/12/1966	-	31/6/1969.
6) Senayangba Ao	1/7/1969	-	7/12/1971.

The head dobashis could rise above the village polity as pioneers in a new system of power aggregation, that could hold sway not only over their village or tribe, but over other tribesmen too. In actual practice, they proved to be the main executors of government policy aside from their actual duty of intepretation. They were the main probe and link to the public for administrative adjudication and the conduit to the official for the masses. Ultimately, they could by personal merit advice and guide the administrator in his function.

The head-dobashis as new-power holders were also reportedly far sighted enough to take advantage of the new social develoment. In the monetised situation, they could avail chances to earn more besides their pay, by engagement in government contract undertakings. As such they could also avail educational benefits for their progenies recognising its importance. It is also in the dobashi institution as a case of development – are identified the emergence of tribal neo-rich people aside from being power holders. Further in their progenies are identified the contemporary power elite and members of the high economic class. In the rise of such sections of the Naga people are conceived the concretization of contemporary Naga social formations.

Ever since the formal organization of the *dobashi* institution in 1914, the function of the dobashis were not merely to interpret official communication but also to interpret customary laws which are unwritten and remain yet to be codified. Having the judicial aspects added to their function enhanced their prominency. The 1935 Court Reforms Act further ratified their position and function which included trial of criminal cases of the tribals with reference to the Code of Criminal Procedure 1898 (Yaden, L.L. Nagaland Code. Vol. 1. 1970:163). The function of the *dobashi* court have been greater magnified and clarified by the Govt. of Nagaland through the Assembly Act of Nov. 1982.

Mokokchung town as an arena of more sophisticated politics can further be illustrated in the formation of the Lotha and Ao Tribal Councils in 1923 and 1928 respectively. Mokokchung being the administrative centre for both the tribes besides it being the community focal point, the office and function of these Councils were centered here. Prominent members of these Councils were *Chansomo Lotha* (later head *dobashi*), *Elibemo Lotha* (later school teacher), *Imkongmeren Ao, Senkalemba Ao* (later head dobashi)etc. The Councils were found to express tribal solidarity. They proved to be sources of interest aggregation of resentment against the colonial rule and a source of intra-political identification of the Naga tribes.

Mokokchung as an arena of sophisticated politics can further be identified with the Naga People's Convention. The Second session of the Convention was held at Ungma village, a satellite of Mokokchung of 3 Km distance in 1958. The Third session of the Covention was held in Mokokchung in 1959 (Yonuo, A. 1974:229). The Conventions marked Naga people's quest for a solution to their political problems, in which the political capacity of Mokokchung as an urban centre is evinced in the personalities like Dr. Imkongliba Ao (Chairman of the Naga People's Convention), Mr. Tekasosang Ao, Mr. Lakimong Lotha, all residents of the town.

With the above discussion, the factor of towns as an arena of politics reflecting Naga unity, Mokokchung town presents a case of Naga social transformation and development. It also proved a case of overshadowing the village societies in total, the formation of a new political structure where the rural backdrop would merely serve to be an appendage of the process of urban politics in the name of total tribal interests.

CHAPTER-V

NAGA ETHNICITY AND IDENTITY

The foregone chapter brings out several crucial aspects. As a case of internal transformation, urban centres, emerged as a service network, began to divide the hitherto entirely rural society into a novelplane of location. As a consequence, these centers came to assume the focal position in the Naga society. However, it may be noted that urban growth in the Naga social experience was not as a result of surplus generation from within or of industrialization, but as a case of colonial administrative presence. The service and avenues generated by urban growth in terms of new occupations and market activities had bearings on the encounter with the capitalistic mode of then British India. Eventually, the Nagas and their internal production dynamics succumbed to the capitalistic mode and its productive process tended to be a parasitic unit of the latter. This aspect is identified as the emergence of a stage of social formation in comparison to the traditional self productive village communities. The gradual development of this dependent syndrome illumines the matter of contemporary Naga socio-economic situation, described as a case of sponsorship, which shall be subsequently examined in this chapter.

Another aspect is the dynamic development of a Naga identity, resultant to the process of uniting discrete tribes into that of one collectivity. This development reflected its frame in the light of the British colonial establishment and later, with that of the Indian Union. It altogether geared the Naga ethnicity in political terms with its own ideology. With its own distinct Naga identity within the Indian Union, a situation has reached in which their relation may be termed as a case of centre-periphery syndrome. This is evident in terms of demography, economy and politics, besides its physio-geographical placement at the extreme eastern end of the Indian Union. As such the ethnic character of the Naga society and its reflection as opposed to the Indian social system gains prominency in the frame of multi-ethnic plurality. In the framework of ethnicity, the Naga society may be described as finding a reflection in the subjective /interactional approach to ethnic studies. In this aspect, analogy maybe drawn from the study of Pathans of North-West Pakistan, wherein membership and identification to the community within a territorial boundary, constitutes a requirement (Barth, F. 1969:117-134). Similarly, as a case of ethnicity, the Naga society is an example reflecting community membership as a matter of identification within its mountainous geographical boundary.

Another analogy maybe drawn from the objective/multi ethnic approach to ethnicity. Here the emphasis is on cultural factors determining the nature of an ethnic group within a wider conglomeration of ethnic groups, thus leading to a plural society, much applied to South-Asian studies (Furnival, J.S. 1939). India represents a classic example of plural society, determined by diverse ethnic groups, where the Naga society on its cultural basis attains qualification of an ethnic status. This includes social values and institutions of the population concerned, serving as demarcating factors.

The ideological or sociology of dependence approach to ethnicity equally qualifies the case of Naga ethnicity. It is primarily based on the Peruvian model of domination and dependence, in which a network of interrelated dependency is established, reflecting unequal power, wealth and status (Verghe, Van Den. P.L. 1975:71-83). In the same vein, reflecting on the Naga and larger Indian society, the latter represents a factor of the dominant role. Added to it is nature of dependency between the two, with the Naga society identified as a consumer-market. The unequal character between the two needs no explanation. The concept of centre-periphery qualifies application here as it were.

The case of Naga ethnicity is a magnified situation as a result of several dimensions. The political movement is one that it generated in search of solidarity, which necessitates examination. This gains credence in contra-distinction to the Indian political process and the constitutional arrangement. Added to it is the economic structure, which in reflection of traditional Naga subsistence economy, now is a case of being prodded up as a viable entity, clearly a case of sponsorship by the Indian economy. This has wider implications of underdevelopment of a community in the light of development of the larger Indian social system.

Consequently, the Naga social reaction in various forms attains a note of interest in terms of its claim of own rights and assertion through constitutional arrangements and other social mechanisms. These are actions in the light of self-appraisal and reflection of its place as a constituent in the Indian federation. This paves the way, in ramification in the generation of Naga identity. This merits study in the light of political and economic dimensions, the expression of its ethnicity in the light of shared historical experiences: Such a derivation in analysis would be clearer in examining contemporary social formations, discerned in the form of class and political elites. This further garners discussion eventually, as to the nature of Naga society as an ethnic society as an ethnic status group and the matter of its social identity.

The study consequently is fraught with elements of polemics, which without drawing closed conclusions will be better understood as a matter of relativity in the light of a participant observer. The essence would be to strike a balance, however tenuous, to explain the complexities of perspectives, when assailed by numerous angles of approach. The major focus of the study would be to dwell on the dimensions of contemporary Naga social formations and the expressions of the community's ethnic identity in the frame of social development.

The Political Factors

Preceded by a discussion on political/administrative consequences of colonial rule (chapter 2), we continue the study here in the light of political development through the early part of the Ninteenth Century. If the urban centres and the rise of the institution of Dobashi served as landmark of power aggregation on a wider and consolidated scale, the establishment of the Naga Club (1918) was an expression of social and cultural solidarity of the Naga tribesmen (Das, N.K. 1982:42). It was reportedly composed of educated and representatives of various occupations, to auger the spirit of unity, manifest of the elements of social perseverance and continual cohesion.

For all its claim of cultural and social basis, its action and relation to the Simon Commission (1928) for statutory reforms study was clearly political, expressing Naga desires to be left alone to determine their own future, in the wake of the British Government quitting the hills and its control. Considering the time and situation, it was anti-colonial and clearly, a speedy fostering of political consciousness, besides overt expression of their political desires. It was then the only organization, theoretically involving most of the Naga tribes. As early as this, the signs of ethnic expression and a form of political development is evident, considering the foundation that ethnocentricity and political development are invariably linked (Somjee, A.H. 1982:8-10).

In the Naga Club's representation to the Simon Commission, a cohesive action for political objectives was identified and further described as a Naga renaissance (Yonuo, A. 1974:126). In essence, it was an honest expression of its anxiety, a paranoia with tangible foundations later, for perseverance against odds. It carried overtures of socio-cultural engulfment, economic fears of undue taxation and deprivation of ecological resources, supersession of their customary laws, customs and traditions and therefore, to leave the Nagas alone "to determine for ourselves as in ancient times (Ibid)". It laid the foundation of Naga political movements and not in the least, the expression of the Naga identity as a people (Das, N.K. 1982:43).

Much as the Naga Club be-spoke of its people's unity, it had its precedence in the form of tribal councils from as early as 1923 and 1928 for the Lotha and Ao tribe respectively, which despite other reasons for its formation, was *per-se* a resource pool of tribal expression in persuance of their aspirations. It was a step in the direction of consolidating the ranks of each particular tribe, finally culminating in the Naga Hills District Council (April, 1945). If in the Naga Club was an ignition of the People's political aspirations for self determination, then in the district council was the convergence of most of the tribesmen in asserting their claim. In it, under the ambit of political articulation, could be perceived the emergence of a total Naga identity; of a small ethnic group closing ranks for self preservation viv-a-vis the larger entity that the colonial power represented. This has corroborating basis considering that it is the colonial factor which provides the motive force in beginning the process of political development with ethnicity as a overriding issue with most underdeveloped and developing societies (Organski, F.K. 1965).

The Naga District Council evolved into the Naga National Council (NNC) in 1946 (Aram. 1974:82) as a form of objective concretization or political medernization. It was not merely a change in nomenclature, but a change in form and outlook, as it was fraught with notions of Naga nationhood (Das, N.K. 1982:42). It was now a larger assertion of being not only an ethnic minority, but of being a nation in the vast link of nationalities the Indian nation then represented. The N.N.C. in the prevailing political atmosphere, proved a nexus of Naga nationalism. They objected to the British- Indian design of a proposed "crown colony", comprising of the North-East frontier Agency (N.E.F.A., now Arunachal Pradesh), a part of Burma and the Naga Hills, supposedly with an aim of ensuring a better deal for the Nagas; declaring that the "British must quit the Naga hills, when they quit India (Alemchiba, M. 1970: 66)".

The Naga people's political objectives and the changes voiced by the N.N.C. can br understood through several phases. At first, their desire was for greater autonomy with special safeguards under the Indian Union on the basis of a 4 Point Agreement, Wokha Conference, 19/6/1946 (Alemchiba,M. 1970:68). Matters however changed when the N.N.C. appealed for an Interim Government under Indian guardianship for a period of ten years and, thereafter, to decide for their own government. This was expressed in their memorandum to the Governor General and the Tribal Advisory Committee, 1947 (Ibid). This was based on their fear of being swamped by the larger Indian population and its culture. In their fear and anxiety, understandably was the inner mechanism of fanning and solidifying their ethnic feelings and political resolve.

A respite seemed at hand by the auspices of the 9 Point Agreement, June/1947 between the N.N.C and the Indian Government- represented by Sri Akbar Hydari, Government of Assam. This did not concretely materialise, with the N.N.C. opting for full sovereignity and to that effect, ultimately declaring Naga independence on 14/8/47. A plebescite followed in 1951 organized by A.Z. Phizo, President N.N.C. on the question of Naga independence. It was claimed to be a success. Later, in 1952, the first General Election of free India occurred, which was successfully boycotted by the Naga people (Das,N.K. 1982:45). One may read Naga political resolve and assertion of ethnicity in these efforts. In 1954, the formation of the *Khunuk Kautang Ngeukhum*_(People's Sovereigv Republic of Free Nagaland) was announced, which later in 1956 was renamed the Naga Central Government. Throughout this period, violence and death marred the situation, because of armed conflict between the Indian and the Naga Army of the N.N.C.

Much harried by violence and motivated by other ideas and objectives besides peace, a split occurred in the N.N.C. One faction led by A.Z. Phizo carried on the armed struggle, while the other faction under J.P.Jasokie, Aliba Imti etc., favoured a middle ground of internal arrangement through non-violent means. Accordingly in 1956, the moderate group affected the Peace Organization Committee helped by the Christian church, ultimately culminating in the Naga People's Convention (N.P.C.), under the chairmanship of late Dr. Imkongliba and Mr. J.P.Jasokie as Secretary. The first session of the Convention affected the amalgamation of the Naga Hills District and the Naga Hills Tuensang Area in 1957. The Convention's second session sought for peace and a political settlement with A.Z. Phizo's faction of the N.N.C. The 3rd session (Mokokchung 1959) desired that the Naga Hills and the Tuensang area be made a state into the Indian Union, supervised under the External Affairs Ministry, the Government of India.

Accordingly, 16 Point Agreement was reached with New Delhi. Through this agreement (most of which is embodied in Article 371-A of the constitution and which gives the Naga society a special constitutional sanction), an act of Parliament was passed in 1960 and the state of Nagaland in 1963 was carved out as the 16th unit of the Indian Union.

It is of pertinent interest as to the nature of the split in the Naga political movement, with the formation of the Naga People's Convention in the frame of political development. Beginning with the Naga Club through the Naga Tribal Council, the N.N.C. as an organised entity for self determination, the majority of the people's support being with them was without doubt, since the party's function and contacts were mainly from the villages. The rural support for the leadership of A.Z. Phizo and Imkongmeren of the N.N.C. then is described as unflinching.

However, for many reasons, the formation of the Naga people's Convention (N.P.C.) in 1957 represented altogether a different political culture. Besides other representatives, this forum also included 60 Naga government employees in various capacities, serving with the government of Assam, the North East Frontier Agency and the government of India (Yaden, L.L. 1970:1). They proved to be an institutional development in the context of change, identified here as the urbanised middle class. Such outgrowths are conceptualised as a result of contact with the social ideals of a larger or developed society and territory, as is the experience of Africa and South-East Asia with Europe and in the case of the Nagas, the larger Indian society (Heeger, A. Gerald. 1974:6). Their outlook and visions were different to that of Mr. Phizo. It is their leadership that the Naga populace could be made to change their views of a Naga nation to that of unity with India. Notable functionaries of this forum were Late Dr. Imkongliba, Mr.J.P. Jasokie, Mr.Vizol, Mr.S.Chubatoshi Jamir, Mr. Kevichusa, etc.

Through the formation of the N.P.C., the state of Nagaland eventually came into being. It marked two different political paths among the Nagas. The N.N.C. led by Mr. Phizo pursuing the path of armed struggle for independence; the other, the N.P.C. stood for the Nagaland as a unit of the Indian Union and thereof its integration with India. In later developments, the N.N.C.and its armed struggle came to an end through the Shillong Accord of 1975 with New Delhi, agreeing to find means to settle the issue with satisfaction on both sides. That accord, contemporarily is observed and criticised as a mere scrap of paper, with the activity of th N.N.C., a feeble force compounded by Mr. Phizo's death and the remnants of the N.N.C. split into two camps namely the Adinno and Panger camps, each claiming the true leadership. The Naga political movement at present remains divided with the emergence of the National Socialist Council of Nagaland (N.S.C.N.), in 1980 a breakaway faction from the N.N.C., pursuing the paths of total independence led by Mr. Isaac Swu and Mr. Muivah. Matters took another turn when the N.S.C.N. divided into two factions, the other being led by Shri Khaphlang in 1988.

In present analysis of Naga politics vis-à-vis the Indian Union, the society presents a case of periphery to the Indian centre. It has a sound basis in the constitutional arrangement. The Article 371-A of the Constitution incorporates (No.7 by Act of the Parliament) the 16 Point Agreement which states that "No act of law passed by the Union Parliament affecting the following provisions shall have legal force in Nagaland." This particularly applies to religion, social practices, customary laws and ownership and trandfer of land and its resources.

The above provisions are a measure of autonomy granted to the Nagas in dealing with local matters peculiar to themselves. It is also observed that through these measures, they have been largely able to attain their objectives short of independence, for their immemorial rights over themselves and resources have been honoured. This in consequence aside from the factor of integration with the Indian Union, proves to be a mechanism of isolaiton (though not by design), out of the national process of political, social and cultural fusion.

Added to it is the factor of scheduling the Nagas as a tribal minority and, therefore, following the policy of the reservation in matters of representation and employment as provided in the Sixth Schedule of the Constitution.

It restricts their right and claim through personal competition and merit. Such favoured treatment and protectionism (though for many legitimate reasons) only heightens their sense of differences from the rest and, thus, flame their ethnicity. Further in reviewing current factors, the state of Nagaland is represented by a lone member in the Lok Sabha (the Indian federal Parliament), whose presence and contribution either by dissent or conformity to national affairs is evidently negligible as compared to the other states and their parliament members. It is argued that the lone membership in the federal parliament is a contradiction to the national claim of all the units being equal, when other states are represented by lagre numbers and possess a decisive force of influence to arbitrate over national policies. For these reasons, aside from the internal political culture, the Nagas remain peripheral to the Indian national political culture, as a whole.

Further as a unit of the Indian Union, the political process within the Naga society is greatly overridden by the idea of "regionalism". This is a concentration on above all political considerations, the idea of self preservation in cultural, social and religious terms, notwithstanding the provisions in the constitution. This appears to be a case of self alienation from the concept of national unity, which serves to heighten the feeling of ethnicity and the identity of being something different, in fact, seen as a case of 'Nagaism'. It is perhaps reflective of the Naga fears and anxieties experienced since colonial times, a matter of the psyche, as if to say that the present situation ia a case of neo-colonialism in a different guise. Such feelings may find support in terms of religious factors that the Naga society is largely Christian, a very small percent of the huge Indian populace. It reflecta an attitude to confine the Nagas to a region , in fact, to the territory it inhabits, expressed in political terms of self-estrangement, true to the definition of regionalism (Mathur, P.C.1983:2).

Most of all, the idea of Naga independence as an ongoing process is perpetuated by the National Socialist Council of Nagaland (N.S.C.N. IM & K) and the Naga National Council (NNC). This provides a cue for the Nagas to vacillate between two political extremes of Indian national integration and Naga tribal independence. This tendency magnifies the ethnocentric focus much vocalized as a measure of identity and political leverage. In review, Naga political movements as a case of development and emerging ethnic identity is observed as a combination of diverse elements, particularly of cultural and social factors, translated through political means (Das, N.K. 1982:48). It is reduced to the point that for all the Nagas stand to be today as an ethnic group within larger India, their experiences "are unique in having an almost entirely political foundation (Elwin, V. 196:70)."

In the review of Naga political process particularly of the objectives of the *Naga Club*, the *Naga National Council* and now with the *National Socialist Council of Nagaland* (IM & K), the factor of ethnic nationalism is an established one. In the light of the frame put forward by Roy Burman, the idea of *infra-nationalism* may be identified with the village republics of pre-colonial days. With the advent of British colonialism, the idea of *proto-nationalism* may be identified with Naga ethnic politics and later in the post-independent era, of *nationalism,* aimed at total independence. Following the political agreement and integration with the Indian Union, Naga ethnic politics may now be identified as a case of *sub-nationalism,* heightened by their assertion of social identity as a people apart from the rest of the people of the nation in terms of culture, religion etc. (Burman, R. 1972:72-97).

Further, Amalendu Guha identifies tribal nationalism (i.e. the case of the Naga and Mizo politics) as a case of reaction to Assamiya language and cultural chauvinism (in this case as representing larger Hindu India). He presents India *as a mixed multinational society*, where big, *small, dominant and non-dominant,* nationalities constitute the union. In the preponderence of a big or dominant unit (i.e. more often the Hindu chauvinism as he puts forward), social movements are generated in reaction as a matter of *spiritual and ideological* stand. Since each unit constitutes a nationality, the force of nationalism of the unit involved gains assertion. Provided the state of the union is not adversely affected, such ideological movements are identified as *little nationalism,* particularly in the context of Naga, Mizo and recently of Asamiya politics (Guha, A. 1981, Feb., April and May E P W.).

Social Consequences of Naga political movement.

In further analysis of the Naga political impasse, to the Government of India it is an insurgency of anti-national proportion while to the Nagas, active in the quest for political independence going with recent vocalization of their issue, it is a liberation movement. It is not the exercise here to examine the veracity of the two opposing views and there-of stand. What cannot be ignored nor wished away are that of the social consequences arising out of it during the last fifty-plus years.

The general Naga public, more so the rural population from the 1950's have suffered the most in terms of deprivation, loss of lives, economic destruction and the ongoing absence of a daily routine sense of order, being sandwiched between the Indian Army and the militants. On a larger degree of tumult, in the 1980's, when the militants began to seep out of the jungles and the distant location of Myanmar to maintain presence and activity in the villages and towns to the attraction of Indian Army response, the obvious consequences were of a higher magnitude of suffering and loss. Sans the gory details irrevelant to the discussion now, here is observed a unique case study of a society, battered and bruised by opposing and differing forces all these years, which have resiliently maintained their social cohesion of differing tribesmen as one Naga community; within that of Nagaland state and thus the Naga identity have not paled or differed in the socio-cultural dimension, as generally happens in other politico-ethnic situations. However in matters of their political view individually within their tribal-social fold, field studies indicate that they more or less, as a matter of long experience and personal understanding, maintain an ambivalent attitude of equi-position to all the forces, long as they are not victimised or affected for one reason or the other. It could be read as a case of owing no allegiance/opposition nor ill will/well wishing stand to nobody or group. This appears to have been over the years, conditioned into their mind set – of the necessity to maintain a fine balance, without any undue tilt to any camp or direction. As a sizable number of respondents in the field put it, it is an arduous exercise of walking the razor's edge.

In contrast to the above within the Naga militants, a contra-distinction is observed and precisely, an inner contradiction, which is that of the hostile opposition to each other of the various factions in quest of Naga political independence, each with the claim of being the bona-fide group representing all the Nagas. To reprise, we trace their political ideology to the Naga Club (1918), later the emergence of the Naga National Council (N.N.C.= Federal Government) in 1946, which is now splintered into the N.N.C. (Panger) and N.N.C. (Adinno Phizo) faction. Out of the erstwhile N.N.C., emerged the National Socialist Council of Nagaland (N.S.C.N. = Govt. of the People's Republic of Nagaland [G.P.R.N.]) in 1980, which further split in 1988 into the N.S.C.N. (I.M.) and the N.S.C.N. (K). The competition between them in the assertion of their bona-fides as the genuine-legitimate faction have also led to a violent turf war. The consequences had been that over the years, large is the casualty list of those killed in action, proving to be a war within a war. The psychological consequences of this trauma to the kith and kin, who constitute the general Naga public would certainly prove to be of significant study.

Another continuing contrast to all of the above is that when it comes to the matter of Indian constitutional assembly elections, as amply proved in 2003, the Naga electorate exemplified dexterous exercise of democratic franchise, in that they were well involved in the election campaign of representation and support to various political parties ranging from regional (Naga People's Front) to several national parties such as the I.N.C., B.J.P., J.D., S.P. to name some. The fact that the state legislative assembly is an undeniable extension of New Delhi and as a parallel to the various factions of the Naga political movement throws much light upon the ability and fortitude of the Naga electorate and the general public at large in their day to day political affairs.

Distilling out more from the above, it is clearly discerned that a dual form of government exists in the Nagaland state contemporarily. To these, the Naga public have to respond and react suitably and as per their ability, walking the razor's edge and maintaining balance between the pulls of the heart and the mind – as a respondent dramatically put it to describe the diametrically different constitutional state authority and the militant's authority. Of this in a parrallax view of political economy, for both the authorities – one is directly funded by New Delhi for all developmental process and maintainance on the proceeds of which – the other finds sustenance.

The general public also proves to be not exactly malleable or passive to events and matters,being long exposed to uncertain passage of years and fissile situations. In matters of excesses, they are vocal and reactive, as with the case of direct confrontation with the Indian Army, involving the National Human Rights Commission over the Mokokchung incident of 27th December 1994. Such reactions are equally meted out to the Naga militants as can be discerned out by the August 2003 incident again at Mokokchung, when owing to public ire, the N.S.C.N. (K) cadres and office, maintaining resident presence were by force evicted out. These are token examples of how the public mind set can coalesce and mobilise in extremities. Such trends are an ongoing phenomenon all over the Nagaland state reflective of the growth of conscious public fury generated over years of humiliation, deprivation and untold suffering, all simmering within, waiting to be vented when events disrupts their tenuous sense of security.

Another obvious consequence have been of daily life being filled with a degree of angst – of becoming a casualty to bullets of one or family. Thus daily life is always filled by a sense of urgency, to complete one's task at hand at the speediest and reach the so conceived security of home. The fallout had been that govt establishments had been so affected owing to early departures by the personnel telling upon efficiency and output. In particular the daily commercial hubris in the urban centres have been so hard hit by market timings being altered to the detriment of profit growth. Thus market commerce begins by the first light of day to conclude by early afternoon. With the shutters down in the shops, the offices empty and the streets deserted, most towns in Nagaland wear abandoned mute looks.

For the reasons above, socio-cultural life as such have been greatly disrupted. Naga tribesmen and their social lives revolve around face to face encounters and interaction, through the process of visitation to each other's homes, after the daily grind. These are not simply for gossip or mere banter – it has a role of affirmation of familiar, kinship and friendship ties. It also seals agreements, creates communication and generates interaction as a matter of cultuiral education and maintainance of it there-of. In these matters, modern means of the telephone or other means of communication have no significance as they are considered impersonal. Other forms of rest and recreation like the cinema, are more or less non-functional. Cine-goers generally are an evening clientele or an afternoon crowd during holidays and sundays. Contemporarily, this form of leisure is a casualty, such that most movie halls in Nagaland are now either shut down or running poor. Rest and leisure in a bar or dinner in a restaurant are now restricted not by law but by the prevailing sense of fear, uneasiness and uncertainty. As a result, it was said by a large number of urban respondents that most of the Naga general public are now turning out to be couch potatoes of being fixed to the video screen and becoming inveterate alcoholics, being confined indoors owing to the out-home air of insecurity. A caustic remark of a respondent was that this is the only game in town – of video and alcohol, particularly in a state with prohibition.

The economic dimension is one which have been hardest hit by the Naga political problem. Most Nagas are claimed Christians constituting 95% in Nagaland. Thus as Christians, it is their religious duty as elsewhere around the world, to pay 10% tithe of their monthly earnings to the Church. In addition to this every Naga wage earner in the state pay taxes to the various militant factions, regarding which a general picture is provided herein:

1) Annual Rs.1 membership fee of every Naga.
2) Annual house tax and army collection ranging between Rs.120 – 50 for both categories.
3) Annual public collection (for civilian cadres).
4) Emergency collection (according to needs and situation).

Besides these, there are vehicle – trucks taxes leading to a wide net of taxation (Sashinungla, Nagaland Page dt. Dec 22nd–23rd 03). At a total picture, it is echoed as per the Ministry of Home Affairs (M.H.A.) 2001, that the N.S.C.N. (I.M.) alone anually crosses Rs. 1500 million through various forms of taxation. Here imagine the grand total gross collection of all the factions combined – it would be astronomical! The overall effect of all these is that to a single household monthly, out of a hypothetical Rs.100, 70 gets deducted as a result of complying to all the taxes. It wouldn't take much to imagine the consequences on individual family lifestyle and conditions.

The above has further ramifications. The commercial sector, either run by Nagas and non-Nagas are equally subjected to taxation. Here it would explain that to defray the cost of these taxations, commercial proprietors merely have to increase the cost price of every item on their counter, taking into consideration their profit margin and the rate – amount of taxation to be deducted. The biggest victim in this is the average customer, that constitutes the consumer section of the Naga economy.

As an off-shoot of the above, even state government departments, as stated in the field are not exempt. Any developmental programme and budget are subject to such taxation. Understandably, these are grey areas where no confirmation, affirmation or verification would be available to its veracity. Likewise contractors and suppliers to gov't tender are equally subject to taxation, the percentage depending upon the amount of their bill, as stated by some in this profession.

The consequences of the prevailing political air upon the youth at large within Nagaland state craves much attention. For one, school- college dropouts for whatever reasons and the unemployed are by way of their un-attached situation, are most suspect in the eyes of the law and authority, particularly the army. Simply proving their bona-fides and legal status to the agents of state authority and the military many a times are confidence losing/resentment growing experiences as and when it occurs. Conversely, they are equally prey to the patriotic call and recruitment drives of the underground forces, on the promise of adeventure and heroism, duty and sacrifice to nation.

Thus, the most pertinent question about Naga youths today are for those who are educated and unemployed. This, in the light of the special constitutional status Nagaland enjoys – is directed toward the state and the central gov't of how concerned they are for the plight of these youths; placed against the ongoing gov't schemes of youth development and problem alleviation which in the youth's view does not meet their emotional expectations. Under the same scrutiny, the other picture is that for these youths in question, what does the Naga independence movement mean for them? For to simply join the rank of the insurgents as mere soldiers, do not exactly meet – much less satisfy their expectations, let alone ignite their sense of Naga patriotism. They represent a significant section of Naga society, who politically and economically speaking, belong to the "twilight zone" as a caustic and cryptic young respondent retorted.

Economic Sponsorship

Simultaneous with the upsurge of Naga nationalism and thereof the interest instilled in the national leadership toward it, a phase of action was initiated immediately after Indian independence. This was with a view to make amends for neglecting the Nagas for so long in the past. Consequently, succour was to be provided for their rapid economic and social development.

Besides the genuine interests, this was also possibly to swamp and de-intensify the Naga political outburst. It was at a juncture of unpredictable situations with radical ideas on the part of the Nagas to develop a people overnight, their motive being to stem the isolationist tendency and anchor themselves to the national concept. As it were, it was time (despite 70 years of British rule), when the land did not register any tangible signs of physical affluence in the villages, much less in the urban centres like Kohima or Mokokchung which were mainly administrative headquarters (Rustomji, N. 1983:52).

The generous attitudes of the Indian Union to develop the people at an unprecedented rate, was in recognition to the fact that the colonial rule was the principal reason for the tribal underdevelopment. This proposition may be a debatable issue. In as much as the Nagas were undeveloped (which *per-se* is a matter of relative ascertainment), the tribals were also in a state of sufficiency, however, subsistent that might have been. What was missed in that picture of social undevelopment in material terms, was that of the idea of political solidarity, generated through 75 years of the British rule and through the ideas and benefits of education, exposure to international Christianity and experience of democracy.

In the internal manifestations stated above, latent with ideologies that crossed the tribal horizon in nature and greater still, nurtured by the claim that the Naga people were not a participant to the national convention and process under British rule for an Indian Union, implied some consequences. These were the lack of constraint and reflection in the face of the development that ensued on the economic plane.

As with the above for credence, "the country (or society) that is more developed only shows to the less developed the image of its own future" (Marx, Karl. Vol.1, Preface). Thus, in the national intentions (of the Indian Union) for the development of the Naga tribals, however noble, were opened the floodgates of disruption (to their indigenous traditions), reflective of the national condition (Rustomji, N.1983:52). Infected with an obsession on the part of the Nagas and supplied without restraint on the part of the Indian Union, many an element of non-tribal higher culture as N. Rustomji (1983:51)cryptically describes and alien to the tribals, were imported and which later affected the society like a malignant contagion.

To illustrate the case of India's economic sponsorship and the consequent emergence of underdevelopment, the Central aid in the form of finance and grants (drawn from the consolidated fund of India), were utilised without rational control. It was fraught with misuse, mismanagement and unjustified spending. In the name of 'developmental projects' so much finance was freely invested as N. Rustomji recounts (1983:520) at exorbitant rates, on the basis of artificial and fictitious market prices. All these led to a situation in which generating of undue-profits, was considered a normal measure of earning and a new style of livelihood. With such a culture of generating profits off public interests through dubious means, the tribals were, as described, displaced from the value of hard work related to proportianate results in terms of production. Here, it was an outright negation of the economic philosophy that with economic development, wealth filters down to all, which further breeds wealth for all.

Of the above, it evolved into a vicious cycle, involving the contractors, the technocrats and the bureaucrats with the blessing of the political decision makers from the above. This explains for the anomaly in distribution of assets and the socio-economic imbalances within the Naga society. It gave birth to a network that operates between the contractor and the legislator, with the technocrat/bureaucrat acting as the conduit and the broker, profiting all involved. Of a survey of 265 politicians over the years, encompassing party functionaries, senior members, legislators (past and present) including ministers, all of them carried a record of being an astute contractor/businessmen by profession. Of these things, it was the opinion of many respondents that political leadership in the state is not determined by quality, commitment and sincerity, but by the amount of money invested in attracting votes.

Such social phenomenon in the guise of economic development, were confined to the slowly growing urban centres. It would be correct to surmise that the extravagant

Central aid has mainly been concentrated in the urban pockets and thus politically dominant economic class. This further explains for the relative difference of development between the rural and the urban Naga society, despite thirty eight years of favoured attention, the former still maintaining the same 80% of the total populace.

The social implications of this economic sponsorshiphave been the development of a parasitic dependency among the Nagas. Such dependence began with the early Naga leadership placed at Kohima, which has now gradually seeped down to all the units of the Naga society at large. The greater implications are that of contemporary social formations of new class and elite strata of the society different from the traditional ethos and, in a manner, peculiar to it. These newly emerged categories are flaunted on the name of mobility and progress.

On the premise that social development is measured in terms of the expenditure incurred, a position which leaves much to be desired for, we provide the amount spent in Nagaland during the last six five year plan.

Table 1: Five Year Plan Budget Allocation for Nagaland.

5 Year Plan	Amount	Total Revenue
1st Plan	Not available	Not available
2nd Plan	Rs. 3 Crores	//
3rd Plan	Rs. 7.15 Crores	Deficit
4th Plan	Rs. 40 Crores	//
5th Plan	Rs. 83.63 Crores	//
6th Plan	Rs. 210.00 Crores	//
7th Plan	Rs. 400.00 Crores	//
8th Plan	Rs. 844.00 Crores	//

(Basic Statistics, North-East Council 2000)

Table 1 is a reflection of the nature of Naga social and economic development, according to the expenditure/ investment of the Five Year Plan. The quantum of the money jumps after every five years in an incremental manner. Yet much less the factor of increasing the potential of self generation as a viable economic unitof the Indian Union, the state has run into perennial deficits. By the latest up-dated data, an amount of Rs. 365 Crores have been granted by the Centre to clear deficits (Nagaland Page, 14/1/04). In fact, the caustic crtique of the Naga state of economy is that of a continuing process of deficits. It is admitted that some revenue is generated from several departments of the government like excise, forest, electricity. However, with prohibition in place, there is now no direct revenue in this sector and with the Supreme Courts ban timber felling, this is another where a source of revenue have been stemmed. Currently, the electricity department bemoans the fact of poor bill collection for various reasons and thus it is beset with its own problems of maintainance at the cost of poor power supply. It is thus surmised that they do not generate anything significant even for the cost of the general administration, least of all, to defray the cost of expenditure or investment.

The five year plan allocation reflected earlier is simply a skeletal view of the financial in-flow involved in over 41 years of statehood. The other unseen picture of the scenario are the non-plan expenditures incurred over the years, all borne by the Central dole. In this, if the sum involved under Centrally Sponsored Schemes of diverse developmental programs are included lumped up along with the grants of the North-East Council, the total financial expenses so far for development of the Naga society and economy would be astronomical. There are also the matter of time to time political sops, when Central leaders on visits to the state or region provides out of the way grants, ostensibly of promoting personal political party interests like the Rs. 1050 crore gifted by the Prime Minister in Oct. 2003 (Nagaland Page, Oct. 2003). All these provisions are yet to translate into economic self reliancy of the Naga society – only it has increased the degree of inequality of contemporary class structure. What is ironic to all these is that the current state ministry is already anticipating a Rs. 60 crore deficit come the 2004 March budget session (Nagaland Page, 7/1/04).

Agriculture

The Naga society is pre-dominantly an agricultural one. It is reported that 80.47% of the population are rural and therefore surmised to be agricultural by occupation (Nagaland, Basic Facts 2002). By virtue of it, it would be assumed that grain production to be sufficient, assuming that much have been invested for agricultural production and grain production (Table 2).

Table 2: Nagaland Agricultural Budget and Production.

5 Year Plans	Expenditure	Grain production
4 Plan (1969 – 74)	Rs. 238.64 Lakhs	63,391 metric tonnes.
5 Plan (1974 – 79)	Rs. 489.33 Lakhs	99,700 metric tonnes.
6 Plan (1980 – 85)	Rs. 2,283.71 Lakhs	120,000 metric tonnes.
7 Plan (1985 – 90)	NA	NA.
8 Plan (1992 – 97)	NA	2,27,000 metric tonnes.
9 Plan (1997 – 2003)	NA	3,55,300 metric tonnes.

Source : Statistical Handbook of Nagaland, 2002, Milennium Issue.
Statistical Handbook of Nagaland, 2001.
Nagaland Basic Facts, 2002.
Basic Statistics, North-East Council, 1995 and 2000.

In spite of all the above revelations, the state is grossly deficit in grain production when the state government has to import from the Food Corporation of India, 4226 metric tones of rice (i.e. 50762 m.t. p.a.) and 5950 metric tonnes of wheat (i.e. 71400 m.t. p.a.) collectively every month for public distribution under Below Poverty Line (BPL), Above Poverty Line (APL), Antyodeya Anna Yojana and Annapurna schemes (Directorate of Food and Civil Supplies 2003). The addition to the above of the amount of grains sold (data not available) through the government licensed 360 fair price shops and the 1225 village councils which are also government declared fair price shops provides verification of the state's deficit food production. Still more, are the amounts of grain (data not available) sold through the general retail shops which clinches the issue of the state as being overly dependent upon out sourcing for food without a doubt. Further, this is despite an incremental increase in the areas brought under cultivation in the past 30 years as shown in table 3 (Statistical Handbook of Nagaland, 2000, Millenium Issue).

Table 3: Cultivation in the Post 30 years Area Under

Year	Area under cultivation
1971	84 thousand hectares.
1981	99 thousand hectares.
1991	NA.
2001	2,02,674 hectares.

As against deficit grain production, besides the ecologcal failure for better production, there are other factors involved in that massive failure. Expenditure for agricultural improvement also involves other equally pertinent ancillaries such as the supply of pesticides, insecticide, high yielding seeds, etc. It is in these aspects as reported in the field that finance meant for it never reaches the actual field of the cultivators. It is a practice of deliberate mismanagement, short of calling it gross-corruption. This is one minor example of what actually transpires at large in the state. Leaving aside moral considerations, sociologically it amounts to an inability to properly utilise the available resources.

Livestocks

The Naga society is characterised by high consumptions of protienous diets, particularly meat. Thus, a look into the aspects of livestocks as a case of the economy merits consideration. It is claimed that the Naga society was self sufficient in this aspect before the advent of national developmental schemes. It is further claimed that on account of various developmental programmes, the grazing ground of cattle were drastically reduced. Further, universal education for children affected the tending of cattle, which was at the level of household industry of the village. Thus, many households were forced to dispose off their cattle leading to a drastic reduction in this aspect since the early 1960's, corresponding to state formation and accelerated developments (Dr. Sekhose, Satuo. Director of Veterinary and Animal Husbandry 1984). Here we are presented with a clear case of development of underdevelopment, from a state of relative sufficiency to a state of increasing dependency. This had been aggravating gradually with the increase of population as against dwindling animal resources.

According to a mid 1980's report, the minimum requirement of meat of the state as a protein source works out to 24,500 tonnes anually. However, the state production works out to barely 10,000 tonnes yearly. In the non-availability of proper data, the protein requirement tonnage contemporarily must have grown many folds in consonance with population growth, as against diminishing local products over the years. The state slaughter of livestock for consumption for the past six years works out this way:

Table 4: Number of Animals consumed in Nagaland ('000).

Species Year.	1994-5	1995-6	1996-7	1997-8	1998-9	1999-0
1. Cattle	74	75	81	81	75	84
2. Buffalo	9	9	11	11	13	13
3. Sheep/goat	22	26	30	30	42	33
4. Pig	74	74	78	78	58	64.

Source: Statistical Hand Book of Nagaland, 2001.

Of the above, it is surmised that local production of the animals consumed barely reaches 8% of the total.What this scenario presents within the Nagaland is that of the absence of the social will to generate production. It reflects a case of high conditioning to the attitude of mass consumerism, notwithstanding the fact that the capital spent has no relation to organized state and society's revenue and profits. It amounts to an outright disposal of direct grants meted out from the central fund, to which it has no contribution to make. The picture turns ironic considering the picture of development of the society in terms of education and for all the benefits it stands for, with the absence of initiative and enterprise. A survey conducted indicates the impression that the white collar employees and the business with large scale investments have displaced the essential spirit of enterpreneurship. This has further heightened consumerism in the society.

As explained earlier, such inability to judiciously apply the grants and aid, generated out of the surplus of the economic enterprise of other units of the Indian Union has only given way, to the growth of the contractor-cum- politician strata in conjunction with the bureucrats and the technocrats. They constitute a category of economically powerfully segment of the society. In this way, these educated white collar, politically active are identified as the middle class.

Besides the evident fact of the Naga society's dependence

on the non- Naga part of India's economy, another pertinent feature to add to the problem is the disproportion in terms of working and non-working population. In five successive census of 1961, 1971, 1981, 1991 and 2001 there has been a significant increase in population. So also, the number of working population has grown, but in terms of percentage to the total population, it has been decreasing (Table 5). Corroborating this, we see the successive increase in the nunber of non-working population. This is a reflection of decay within the society-of a larger section being dependent on the labours of a smaller section, despite massive grants and aid from the Centre. It indicates by implication the growth of class characteristics, particularly determined by the failure on the part of the larger Naga society to generate motivation and economic production from within.

Table 5: Population Break-up.

Census	Population	No. of main workers	No. of non-workers	% of workers
1961	369,200	219,310	149,890	59.40
1971	516,449	262,114	254,335	50.75
1981	773,281	354,102	419,179	45.79
1991	12,09,546	5,16,237	6,93,309	42.68
2001	19,88,636	8,49,982	11,38,654	42.74

The parasitic and dependent nature of the Naga economy is indicated by the breakup of the main workers and the non-workers in their current respective categories based on the 2001 Census. The table clearly reflects the growth of dependency by the decreasing pecentage of workers over a span of 40 years. It may be argued that population growth proves to be a drain to the economy to render it dependent. But it could be counter argued that incremental budgetary allotment growth could have propped up the economy to a self sustainable level as to escape the identification of being a parasitic economy and society.

Of Table 6: the cultivators and agricultural labourers represent the section that is clearly marked by under production in economic terms, verified by the import of high grain tonnage and livestock. What is stated as "others" is now surmised to constitute the contractor-supplier and commercial-business section including professionals like doctors-lawyers who by way of their profession are observed to constitute a section of varying degrease of affluence far removed from poverty and penury. The marginal workers represents those that lead a subsistence existence of daily hand to mouth situation. The government employees ranging from Class I-V represents those with the most security of being assured of an income every month (Table 6). They represent the only section to be characterised by a required minimum of education to the highest possible.

Table 6: Breakup of main-workers.

Workers categories	No. of workers	Percentage
1. Govt. employees (Class I-V)	64,517	32.44
2. Cultivators, agri labourers, others	6,43,938	32.38
3. Marginal workers	1,41,527	71.16
4. Total Workers.	8,49,982	42.74

Statistical Handbook of Nagaland, 2001.

The focus on the above further reduces the fact of the situation that of a total population of 19,88,636, only 849,982 constitutes the working population, whose basic income individually with due consideration of the weak economic situation, would be merely subsistent for a majority. And on them, a majority of non-working population remains dependent constituting 11,38,654. In further analysis, that the total population of the Naga society remains dependent on the aid from the Indian Union brings out their dependent nature.

Industry

Prospectively, the Naga economy produces nothing significant for self sufficiency, much less surplus for export and revenue. All items of essential commodities, luxury items, clothings and energy are imported from the other neighbouring state of Assam and the nation at large. For reasons of political slogans of being industrialised, the state once boasted of one paper mill at Tuli, one sugar mill at Dimapur and one plywood factory at Tizit. The paper mill was set up at a cost of Rs.56 crores with a planned capacity of 100 tonnes per day in pulp production. Its production presently is zero, with a large work force, still on the payroll. The sugar mill was setup at a cost of Rs. 4 crores and much less being tasted by the Naga consumers, the factory have been defunct for the last one decade. Having failed to raise any revenue at least to defray the cost of establishment these are now described as "dead elephants". The note of high concern is that the internal economic structure of purchase and sale, acquisition and consumption are all based on cash meted out by the Centre and the consumer goods, all imported from without. To offset the above scenarios as a matter of presentation, a mini cement plant has been under operation ever since 1995, with the production capacity of 50 tonnes per day. The unfortunate comments to this effort is that this pronounced quality cement are not commercially available as desired in the state, nor is it exported to the other states as confirmed. The query is where is the cement? In consequence, all the cash in float and reserve eventually circulates out of the state to its point of emanation, leaving the society emptier and more dependent. And then the cycle of 'development' continues.

Based on the press releases and the publications of the government of Nagaland, allegedly the Naga economy and society at large is in a state of development. This is true in so far as the expenditure incurred is concerned paid for from the Central fund. The picture apparently gets rosy by the increase in road communication, literacy, health and longevity of life, rural water supply and electrification. But these are non-returnable aspects of development, whose combined and total impact by application foster the element of self-generation for tangible social and economic development. However, this is not the case inspite of 41 years of favoured attention. Instead, an exploitative dependency has ensured within the society rendering it in further consequence to be parasitically dependent on the larger Indian society. The whole situation qualifies the conditions of a society who in order to establish that intrinsic capacity to initiate development, in the light of a patron or of a dominant society consequently only ends with the factor of under-development (Frank, Andre Gunder, 1967:32). The analogy may not exactly conform to the Latin-American experience, nevertheless, it amounts to a case of self-underdevelopment in the light of their own ethos, that of the Naga society.

The factor of Naga underdevelopment and its continuing entity of being a part of the Indian economic system is clearly reflective of a sponsored society. Simply, the matter can be reduced to a mere expalnation that at the insatnce of Indian aid being withdrawn, the Naga society will face a collapse. Such growing dependence and its consequent underdevelopment has historical and political reasons, added to reasons of failure to muster strength and motivation to attain its own capacity on the part of the Naga society. This is quite evident in tracing the period of Naga history vis-à-vis the nation after independence. Further, it is also with the consideration that "contemporary underdevelopment is in large part the historical product of past and continuing economic other relations between the satellite underdeveloped and the now developed metropolitan countries" (Frank, Andre Gunder, 1967:32-36).

Thus, added to the Naga socicty's lack of capacity to initiate its own economic growth from within, it would come to acceptance that the Indian policy of tribal development, no less the Naga tribes since independence has initiated the current phenomenon of social underdevelopment. The process is evident from the massive grants and aid meted out hence to-date, particularly motivated by political reasons to stem the separatist attitude of the Naga society. It was an effort to divert attention by lures of easy economic benefits, without considering the absorbtive capacity of the society concerned. It presumably left no room for self appraisal or reflection.

From an overall view, it has rendered the Naga society to the position of a consumer of the products of the Indian economy. It is now the caustic opinion that were anything to happen to the productive side of the Indian economy, the Naga society besides being a consumer, will simply wither away. Such factors only bring out in clearer detail the centre – periphery syndrome of the nation and Naga society.

This has further consequences. It now only heightens the feeling of Naga insecurity as a dependent society, in which they find expression of being a backward ethnic group. Such feelings are further promoted in political terms which in return, accrue greater grants and aid, ensuing the cycle of dependence and underdevelopment still further. It is now a matter of an established cycle, in which the peripheral ethnic Naga society and the core Indian society is inexorably linked; as a market and producer, strengthened by the peculiar political and constitutional link as a political unity, in which neither apparently gains.

In precise terms, considering the nature of the Naga economy with its lack of internal initiative and the paternalistic attitude of the Indian economy, we are presented with a picture of economic sponsorship with many social implications. Its basic roots may be found in the Constitutional status meted out to the Nagas as a scheduled tribe, which was further determined by political considerations to maintain the national integration. And all these have resulted in shaping the Nagas into a sponsored society, cutting its basic roots and evolving none of its own.

In concluding the discussion on this chapter, it would be pertinent to refer to Samuel P. Huntington's ideas of political development and political decay (1975:2-45). He advances that political development has its basis on the multiplication of political demands, which are shaped by the process of social and economic change. Further in the process of political development, traditional political institution and its capabalities to sustain itself are undermined, or as it were, forced to a state of decay by the new process. This involves wider political participation to new goals, with the rational Potentiality of cutting across narrow and local issues. Huntington further states that political, economic and social prowess are strongly related, however, independent their goals may be. Therefore, it is the general understanding that economic development leads to political stability and vice-versa, despite their independent goals (which particularly is the American political belief in shaping their foreign policy towards developing nations).

The Naga political development and its ethnic collectivity in relation to British colonial rule and later the Indian Union, echoes Huntington's views. This may be identified with the process of over-shadowing and, thus, decay of the traditional village polity. However, the case of contemporary Naga political process and status as a unit of the Indian Union may be described as a case of institutional failure in Huntington's frame. This finds application in consideration that Naga political capability as a unit of the Indian Union registers no significant influence or effect in the wider national political and spectrums. This aspect is further aggravated with some section of the Nagas expressing separatist tendencies, reflective of dis-unity within and thus renders their political capacity to be weak. Further, considering Hutington's frame that political, economic and social process are related despite its independent goals, it would appear that political development would invariably lead to socio-economic development. However, the Naga political development has rendered its economy to a state of gross dependence from a state of village self sustenance. All these coupled with the weak institutional political structure and the social frame of entrechment to a static level, the contemporary Naga social formation presents a case more of political decay than that of developoment. The facets of Naga transformation call it development or decay, is more visible in the urban centres. This finally brings us to propose conceptually more, an overview of contemporary Naga social formations in terms of class divisions.

Naga Social Formations- An Overview

History have certainly played a significant role in transforming the Naga society from a stage of traditional inequality to contemporary class emergence of un-equal social relations. Based upon the discussions on economic sponsorship and its consequences discussed earlier, the various occupational categories as now found in the Nagaland state is accepted as the basis of class divisions of contemporary social formations, based upon an economy maintained by the largesse of the larger Indian economy on the sanction of constitutional arrangement. Here, in the identification of the Naga class structure, we are led by Parkin's (1971) contribution that the basis of the modern class structure is the occupational order. In this, the general identification of the middle class as made by Stearns (1979) become a significant utility which further help to identify the higher and the lower, in conceptual and there-of emperical reality.

We take the time here to state that on middle class, the path breaking contributions of Cole (1955) and Misra (1961) are still refreshingly relevant even today.

The occupational order as is found today in the Nagaland state are largely divided into the (1) Government services and the (2) private services. The Government services are characterised by recruitment through the Union Public Services Commission (UPSC) and the Nagaland Public Services Commission (NPSC). For other posts, it is done through departmental processes as and when officially notified. Here, education and there-of subsequent qualifications in other aspects of scrutiny, according to corresponding order of post and requirement ensures the recruitment.The Government service occupational/ professional order are divided into classes as provided in Table 7.

Table 7: Government Services and Class Breakup

	Class I	Class II	Class III	Class IV	Total
No.	2591	916	33,399	27,611	64,517.

Source : Statistical Handbook of Nagaland 2001. (Based upon 1997 Survey).

Of the total 64,517 employees of the government as given above, by the class division which entails corresponding salary, work and responsibility, policy and decision making duties and implementation, from a subjective view of the observer/field examiner, the matter of who is/are upper/ middle/lower class is quite clearly discerned out of that arrangement of work, power, prestige, income and lifestyle configurations.

The private services are distributed among 6,43,938 numbers of the population who are simply described as the main workers, cultivators, agricultural labourers and others (Statistical Handbook of Nagaland 2001). In here would be included the contractors and suppliers, business and commercial entrepreneurs, the professionals like doctors and lawyers, trained and skilled workers to identify a few. In this would also be included the marginal workers who number 1,41,527.

In terms of workers and non-workers of the population in Nagaland, as per the 2001 census, the total working population number 8,49,982 as against a non-working population of 11,38,654, clearly indicative of a bottom heavy dependent section, reflective of a parasitic consumer syndrome.

The Lower Class

The lower class as recent field observation revealed and greatly ratified by respondent's view on being queried as to who would constitute this stratum, stated that the rural population at large numbering 16,00,454 constitutes this class (Basic Facts, 2002, Nagaland). This would mean the inclusion of cultivators agricultural labourers (actual break-up in terms of specific number not available) and a sizable number of the marginal workers earlier stated as numbering 1,41,527. In terms of economic security, most cultivators are characterised by bare sufficiency, meaning there is no surplus. In terms of cash earnings as a result of forest produce, other cash crops of fruits and vegetables, the average income is surmised to range from Rs. 3,000 to Rs. 15,000, which after meeting annual expenses, does not provide them any latitude as to transcend their existential position.

Being placed in the lower class stratum, it would be safe to arrive at the conclusion that the rural population are poverty written in the true sense. They are not landless because even for the poorest of the lot, the community land provides them a dwelling site in the village and cultivation plots out in the fields. Neither are they shelterless because every household have at the least a bamboo-thatch house to be secured in. Contemporarily, Naga villagers are not exactly dark come sundown, as electrification have reached all the villages as claimed, provided there is regular power supply. It is also claimed that most villages have been water supplied by taps, thus transcending the drudgery of transporting water from outside the village stockade and boundary.

In terms of education, there are 1317 villages in Nagaland (2001 census). There are 1491 primary schools distributed in the villages and towns and corresponding higher levels of schools to which several villages are clustered ascendingly (Statistical Handbook of Nagaland 2001). However, the rural population as the lower class, it is the considered opinion of most students hailing from rural backgrounds that anyone above the age of 40 in the villages are illiterate. It however does not mean that those below 40 are literate. Most can barely read in vernacular while writing becomes ponderous.

In the urban centres notably Kohima, Mokokchung and Dimapur to mention some in particular, the lower class obviously are the marginal workers to begin with (here the workers under discussion are all Nagas). Official identification does not specify their break-up in terms of work variety: but most are rural migrants who are mainly illiterate. They constitute the daily wage workers being un-skilled and un-trained. They earn about Rs. 80 a day meaning they barely manage to eke out a living. Others are those possessing a skill through appprenticeship like the construction workers, auto mechanics, electrical fitters, auto-rickshaw drivers and cart-pullers to mention a few who reportedly earn about Rs. 100 a day. There are the petty hawkers and the street vendors who comparatively are decribed to be a few degrees better off than the others.

Most of these low-level working population do not possess their private dwellings. They are thus tenants in tenement structures and shanties. As an exception, some do own their own dwellings on their own plots as a result of having owned more in the past, now most of them disposed off. Owing to indiscrete spending and lack of foresight, they are now reduced to this level of drudgery of daily squeezing out a life. For all of them, it is a life of poverty, dirt and squalor, with no visible sign of a warm future.

The class IV government employees are also lumped up with those of the above, although their conditions are definitely better. They have a minimum education of class VIII-X for which primary reason they are employed. They have a steady monthly income meaning a modicum of security, although admittedly based upon their income, unless there are double earners within the household they are also confined to limited avenues. Of this section, most household respondents indicated possession of modest homes on small plots of land.

The Middle Class

From the private services the identification of this class is first based upon urban place of residence, education and observable lifestyle of relative comfort and consumption. First of all, they are the contractors and suppliers ostensibly of the class II category, along with corresponding commercial businessmen and tradesmen, along with politicians in various party functions including elected legislatures.

From the government services, the class II and III employees starting from middle level bureaucrats and technocrats to supporting staffs of ranked pay division remains a significant section of the middle class. Most are urban based however those in rural postings in comparison with the rural neighbours could even be scaled much higher up, for instance, school teachers, medical dispensary workers, veterinary and agricultural unit workers to mention some. Of this section, within, it could also be possible to identify and rank them in terms of high-middle class, mid-middle class and lower-middle; if we put into consideration, their respective income brackets, decision making processes and execution.

In this category at large, hair-splitting divisions is very much a possibility – although its basis of identification and selection could be arbitarily subjective in the absence of generally agreed upon models of ranking and identification.

The fact remains that all the middle class members have private residences on their private lands in the urban centres. That they lead variable levels of comfortable or adequate lives would not be wrong. That household appliances like t.v. and refridgerators, phone connections etc. requires no mention. That most of them own at least a private mode of transportation from a vehicle – car to a two-wheeler goes without saying. More than as a necessity, it is fashionable within this class to have their children pursue studies outside of the state.

They form a significant section of the Naga working population, who are known for their activism and dynamism, responsible for keeping the institutions in process and being a conduit and link between the various divisions of the social structure. In fact the Naga middle class is seen as an extension of the Indian class situation in whom is clearly reflected the process of Naga social transformation and development. It is this class which have been historically significant in the course of Naga politics specially of the Naga Club (1918) whose members possessed education and represented new occupations and most of all cohesion among themselves (Misra, U. 1983). They represent the educated, propertied and influential section of the Naga society as a substantial part of the urban population of 3,88,182, as against a rural population of 16,00,454 (2001 census). They determine the course of politics and change of government, whose contractors and businessmen represents the neo-rich, a parallel development to the Bhotia plebians of Sikkim (Sinha, A.C. 1975).

The Upper Class

The concept of the upper class as discussed earlier in the introduction involves power, wealth etc. It also reflects the aspect of superiority as against the other strata in the class structure, similar with that of the elite although, the two are conceptually diverse. However, as discussed in the introduction, we further understand that the phenomenon of elite emergence may lead itself to the role of symbolising the process of class formation. It becomes quite clear that the concept of elite is closely and critically lined with that of class. Therefore, empirically, the upper class becomes quite inseperable with the elite, reminescent of the two faces of the same coin. With this understanding, the explanation as provided by Pareto and later, as given by C. Wright Mills, T.B. Bottomore among others, gains credence and application. We apply the same analogy in the case of the Naga society.Therefore, though the social base of the upper class is much larger, in life style they are similar with the elite. There is an obvious overlap between the two.

In the light of the identification of Indian elite as represented by the higher status of the castes on ascriptive basis, a similar analogy can be applied to the traditional Naga society. With the Sema and the Konyak Nagas, their chieftainship (Akekao and Ang respectively) can be identified as the traditional elite. They qualify all the attributes of the elite/upper class characteristics as provided in the theoretical framework. With the Ao and the Angami Nagas, their council of village elders identify as elite. Their positions were not exactly ascriptive, however, their representation of their clan is reflective of their merit and qualities, not common to all.

Contemporary Naga upper class is broadly identified into the *administrative elite, the political elite and the business elite*. The scheme of approach here at large conforms to Bottomore's identification of the "political leaders and the high governement officials" as being the Indian elite (1979: 145). In particular, it identifies with A.C. Sinha's (1975) identification of the elite in Sikkim which serves a practical reference model for the region and further, R.N. Thakur

(1981) and his identification of the Indian administrative elite.

The Administrative Elite. In Nagaland, the admistrative elite is identified with the 2591 Class I government employees. Beginning with the Chief Secretary, it includes all the bureaucrats and technocrats in the secretariat and directorates, spanning the various government departments. They represent the ultimate source of administrative power for the whole state, characterised by prestige influence and high salary. They represent the highest organ of executive power establishment of the government. They represent not merely the execution of policies, but also of political power by function, as they have to by role remain close to the legislature.

Certain matters are brought to light for elaboration. Much as political neutrality is pre-supposed on the part of the admistrative elite (Bottomore, T.B. 19798: 130-8), the boundary between administrative function and political process turns skin deep particularly in the Nagaland. By virtue of it being a small society, all the process of government and politics tend to fuse as one. Further, the administrative elite by function and execution is mainly a reflection of political decisions on larger issues and often it is the administrative elite and their advisory function that determine political decisions

The Political Elite. The political elite of Nagaland projects an image of male leadership as is the case with Sikkim (Sinha, A.C. 1975). Here as in the case with larger India, we identify the elective legislatures who are sixty in number, the party leaders and functionaries as the political elite: representing the Indian National Congress, Nagaland People's Front, Bharatia Janata Party, Samata Party, Janata Dal (U) and Independent Legislative members. At the most, they would constitute in number about a hundred including the two members of parliament one for the lower and the other for the upper house out of a total population of 19,88,636 representing sixteen major tribes.

The above analysis relates and identifies with the political elitc of the total society and state. Of the above, many are retired government servicemen, contractors and businessmen and professionals like lawyers and doctors. There are also those without a modicum of education, who by personal merit and support of kinship ties have attained such positions. This is particularly characterisive of the politicians of the northern most part of Nagaland.

The Business Elite. In Nagaland, this section is identified with the class I contractors and suppliers whose cash values of each undertaking runs in terms of many lakhs to crores. They are very prominent whose yearly income as is reliably reported runs into crores. They are reputed to be experts for any costly and major undertakings, whose business network reaches out to other states of the region and the nation at large.

In politics, their involvement is reportedly deep and decisive. They do not necessarily claim membership to any political party as such, however, they are reportedly connected to the members of the legislative assembly, fielded and financed by them. This in consequence enables them to further and expand their business set up, besides being protected by political patronage. It further keeps them in the arena of political process and exposure, consulted and referred to, always on the advantageous side of an issue. This is reflective of the total Naga society, and as described, having a finger in every pie of the political, economic and social process. In reversing the picture, it comes to identification that the political actors also constitute the Naga business elite. For most practical purposes, the boundary between the two is superficial with many of them.

The elites maintain high and expensive social lives as a reflection of their wealth. Most of them are members of the

Rotary and Lion Clubs. They are also patrons of such sporting and cultural clubs, drama and aesthetic clubs involved in functions and events related to big expenses reflecting glamour and prestige. They are also steady contributers to the Church without necessarily being religious, paying large sums of donations for charitable works and missionary purposes aside from the payment of required monthly tithes as professed Christians.

Most of all, they maintain strong family, kinship and clan ties, taking responsibility for most of their material needs. This, aside from fulfilling traditional norms as a rich person, it has also implications of customs of maintaining blood ties and the network of relations, true to Naga charasteristics. In contemporary times, this factor plays an important function in the election process. This all the more raises their prestige and influence.

CHAPTER-VI

CONCLUSION

The contemporary Naga social formation is identified from the onset of the period of colonial encounter and concretized into the contemporary conditions after the Indian independence. It is a continious process in which the Naga tribals were slipped from their traditional moorings. Much as history explains the colonial encounter as a nominal extension of political control of the larger India (i.e. without actual subjugation and exploitation as is characteristic of the colonial rule), it was fraught with other implications as well. Some of these are read in the contradiction found with the *British policy of non-inteference* in the internal arrangements of the Nagas inhabiting the Naga hills.

To highlight the contradiction in the *policy of non-interference*, the imposition of house taxation on the then Nagas, is identified as intrinsic to the nature of direct control (and of subjugation). This clearly stands out in contradiction. More aptly, it may be described as an indirect policy of subtle interference. It comes to calrity that the policy of non-interference was vainly flaurited to the extent that there was no significant economic exploitation of natural resources in the Naga hills, as was, characteristic with the other colonial locations.

The limited taxation in the form of cash (hitherto non-existent with the Naga tribals), created such a situation in which an average Naga had to work on the British economic institution such as road construction, so that he could earn some cash to pay for the taxation. Howsoever, small it was, it did introduce the elements which transformed the state of the then existing economy. Besides transforming the barter economy of the traditonal Naga society, it in itself proved to be a transition from one formation to another, with the consideration that the nature and state of the economy determines the reproductive process of social formation of a society from one stage to another. To describe the process, it may be viewed in the manifestation of providing an impetus to earn cash, which in consequence diversified the economy in a limited way and also of occupation, as opposed to traditional mono-productive activity of cultivation. With economy as a crucial factor in the study of social formation, the colonial encounter presents a pertinent factor of transformation to another, which explains for the contemporary Naga society.

Added to the factor of economy, the next pertinent factor is that of politics or more aptly in this case, the form of state administrative control in the study of social formations. With colonial encounter, the Naga tribal polity based in the village, and which by itself represented a social formation, was overshadowed by a wider political control. It manifested in the rise of such new institutions as the *dobashis and the gaunboras* (interpreters and village elders respectively), the new agents of the British rule at the local level. The rise of such institutions clearly indicates the extent of Naga subjugation. In course of time, this alien British political control generated new desires and objectives among the Nagas. This was the beginning of Naga identity, transcending narrow and isolative village polity and concern for a comprehensive political future for the community. It spelt out Naga wishes for self rule as one conglomerate body of the various tribal groups and emphasized the Naga solidarity. This aspect manifested as early as 1918 with the Naga Club and later the Naga National Council (N.N.C.) to begin with.

What began with the colonial encounter, the above Naga ethnic expression was further fanned by the new arrangements on the eve of the Indian independence, because it found itself enveloped into the arrangements of the Indian Union. The conflict with the colonial rule was replaced by the Indian Union, with mixed political views and expressions of liberation and secession. After some years of violent encounters, the situation was controlled through a political arrangement of the *Sixteen Point Agreement* between the Nagas and the Indian Union. This finalized the status of the Naga tribals as an integral unit of the Indian Union, with measures of privileges and autonomy granted unlike other sister states. It, however, did not result into the complete unity of the Naga tribals with the Indian nation. One section of the Nagas opted to struggle for total independence led by the Naga National Council (N.N.C.). This factor explains for the peculiar political relation, empathy and ambivalence between the Naga society and the Indian Union.

Colonial control also ushered in the factors of Christianity and education as forces of social transformation, added to the administrative political control and monetization of the economy. These forces represented characteristic units of a new social formation in comparison to the traditional situation. These external forces were instrumental in affecting transition from one stage to another. Christianity gradually displaced the age old belief in animism. The factor of sharing a common and and larger religion proved to be cohesive in uniting the various tribes into that of a larger entity. It could greatly add to their political desires of ethnic distinctiveness.

Education naturally appeared to have widened the mental horizon and capacity of the Nagas. It proved a springboard to enable the Naga society to attain the fruits of learning and share in the wider proliferation of knowledge of the world at large. It did generate Naga consciousness even further in the changed situation. All the more important, education provided a new way out for social mobility and non-traditional achievements. In relation to occupation and income, it proved to be a motivating factor and, consequently, also a basis of contemporary social inequality between the rural and urban sectors and between the urban inhabitants in particular. Education paved the way to social inequality and then class differentiation and even elevating some of them to elitist positions.

The growth of urban centres which emerged out of the then administrative outposts, at first proved to be effective rural/urban market centres. In a very limited way, they turned out to be the melting pots for the various tribals. The case of Mokochung town provides a pertinent example in this context. It proved to be a developing focus of individual enterprise and freedom from the tradition-bound shackles of village centred control by an overbearing chief (i.e. the Konyak and Sema Nagas), or constraints of community will (i.e. the Ao and Angami Nagas). Most of all, it meant the generation of new occupations of non-agricultural nature, revolving around the investment and accrual of cash, through trade and commerce within and with the outside world represented by larger India.

In course of time, the urban centers became the major focal points for the community. It proved to be a superimposition of a source of influence and change from the major rural backdrop. This became significant particualrly with the creation of the state of Nagaland and its implication of organized state control of the society. It became the emanating point of most of the ideas and activities for dispersal to the rural masses. Most significantly, the breakdown of communal feelings of the various tribes for the emergence of a larger Naga identity was made possible in the urban centres through interaction and diffusion. The study of Mokokchung town presents a clear profile of such a success.

At length, the formal integration of Nagaland with the Indian Union meant large inflow of concessions for economic and social development of the society. It finds description as the concretizing process of contemporary social formation, begun with the period of colonial encounter. Economic development of the Naga society also meant besides many other aspects the emergence of elite and class inequality. This is again clear with the inequality between the major rural backdrop and the small urban forefront. It gains greater clarity in the comparative measurement between the urban sections of the privileged and the possessed and the underprivileged and impoverished. Most of all, in the interplay between power politics (i.e. the means of state control) and the economic dimension; with no means of entrance into the power game and ascendency in the economic pasture for those with no prior power reference or economic clout. In the emergence of a larger Naga identity out of the fusion of the various tribes, the internal inequality between classes is characteristic of contemporary Naga social formation.

Further in evaluation, the relation between the Naga society and the Indian Union at large is one of interplay between a weaker periphery and the dominant core. This is evident for one in the political dimension of the Indian National State. Represented by a lone member in the Lok Sabha (Lower House of Parliament), the Naga society's contribution to national policy pales into insignificance.

Another aspect is the state of the economy of the Nagaland. For an agricultural society, the agricultural production of the state is proverbial. In spite of the massive aid poured in, the production infrastructure besides agriculture is virtually non-existent. With the claim of being industralized, its sugar and paper mill are merely 'dead elephants', in the sense that they are not commercially and industrially viable propositions. As for small and cottage industries, these are units yet to make any significance. Most of all, the very social motive to be self generative is nil. In consequence, the Naga society has to depend on the economic productions of the nation at large, paid for in cash poured in by the Centre through the budget allocations for overall development. It is the process of gross diminishing returns on all fronts. This brings out the quality of 'development' against the decay in the traditional social set up. Most worrisome of all is that with the onslaught of globalization, which cannot be wished away, the question abounds as to what happens to small dependent societies and economies in the long run?

In conclusion considering the role of Nagaland in the Indian Union, the former remains peripheral to the Indian system in terms of politics, economy, social structure and religious affiliation. No doubt the erstwhile Naga society has effectively been brought under the orbit of the advanced Indian economy, though contribution of the Naga productive forces to the Indian Central pool is almost nothing. Naturally for its own sustenance and completion of the various state sponsored projects it heavily depends on the Central Government for the support. All these have led to a lopsided development rather a type of decay in the traditional Naga equilibrium and made the Naga society as a unique case of sponsorship, which smacks of inequality, patronage and clientele. Thus, the contemporary Naga social formation exhibits a trend, which indicates a very different course in spite of all the claims of 'development' on the part of the formal structure.

BIBLIOGRAPHY

Amin, Samir : *"Unequal Development (An Essay on the Social Formations of Peripheral Capitalism)"*, Delhi, 1976.

------------: *"Class and Nation: Historically and in the Current Crisis"*. Monthly Review Press, NewYork.

Alemchiba, M.: *"A Brief Historical Account of Nagaland"* Naga Institute of Culture, Kohima, 1970.

------------:"Problems of Re-adjustment to a new Situation." From "Tribal Situation in India" Ed. K.S. Singh. Indian Institute of Advanced Studies, Simla, 1972.

------------: "The Naga Culture". From "The Thinker". Journal of Thinkers Forum. Kohima. 1974, Feb-March Vol.I. No. 1&2.

Ao, Tajenyuba. : "British Occupation of Naga Country" 1993. Naga Literature Society, Mokokchung, Nagaland.

Aram, Dr.:"Peace in Nagaland: Eight Year Story" Arnold Heinemann, new Delhi, 1974.

Bailey, F.G.: *"Caste and the Economic Frontier"*. Manchester University Press, London, 1957.

Bareh, Hamlet. : "Nagaland: Gazetteer of Kohima." Kohima, 1970.

Banton, Michael.: "Urbanization and Role Analysis". From "Urban Anthropology: Cross Cultural Studies of Urbanization. "Ed. Aidan Southhold. Oxford University Press, 1973.

------------: "Racial and Ethnic Competition." Cambridge University Press, London 1983.

Barth, Frederick, Ed. : "Ethnic Groups and Boundaries: Pathan identity and its maintenance". Little Brown. Boston, 1969.

Berreman, Gerald D: "Social Inequality: A Cross Cultural Analysis." In Social Inequality. Comparative and Developmental Approaches. Gerald D. Berreman, ed. 1981. Academic Press. New York.

Betteille, Andre.: *"The Idea of Natural Inequality."* In Social Inequality. Comparative and Developmental Approaches. Gerald D. Berreman, Ed.1981. Academic Press. New York

------------: *"The Idea of Natural Inequality and Other Essays"*. 1983, Oxford University Press.

Bohanon, Paul.: *Social Anthropology.* New York: Holt, Rinehart and Winston 1963.

Bower, Ursula Graham.: "The Naga Path" Oxford University Press. London. 1959.

Bottomore, T.B.: "Sociology: Guide to problems and Literature." Allen and Unwin. 1964.

------------: "Sociology and Social Criricism." Pantheon Books. New York. 1974.

------------: "Classes in Modern Society." George Allen and Unwin. London, 1975.

Burman- Roy, B.K.: "Intergrated Area Approach to the Problems of the Hill Areas." From "Tribal Situation in India." Ed. K.S. Singh. Indian Institute of Advanced Studies. Simla 1972.

Butler, Capt.: "Rough Notes on the Angamis." Journal of Asiatic Society. 1875 Vol. XLIV. No. 4. From "Nagas in the Nineteenth Century". Ed. V. Elwin, Oxford University Press, 1967.

Broom & Selznik.: "Sociology". Harper and Row. New York, 1966.

Clark, M.M.: "A Corner in India." Christian Literature Centre. Gauhati. Reprint. 1978

Chandra, Satish.: "Medieval India: Society, the Jagirdari Crisis and the Village." Macmillan. Delhi. 1982.

Cole, D.H.: "Studies Class Structure." Oxford University Press. London. 1955.

Das, N.K.: "Naga Movement." From "Tribal Movements in India." Ed. K.S. Singh. Manohar Publications. New Delhi. 1982.

Dahrendorf, Ralph.: "Recent Changes in the Class Structure of European Societies."London. 1954.

Elwin, Verrier.: "The Aboriginals." Oxford University Pamphlets on Indian Affairs. Bombay. 1944.

------------: "Nagaland". Research Department, Adviser's Secretariat. Shillong. 1961.

Ehrensaft, Philip.: "The Rise of Photo-bourgeoisie in Yorubaland." Canadian Journal of African Studies. Vol. 13. Montreal 1972.

Fallers, Lloyd H.: *"Inequality: Social Stratification Reconsidered"*. Chicago: University of Chicago Press. 1973. Faris, Ellesworth.

Freidman, Jonathan.: "Tribes, Nations and States." From "Marxist Analysis and Social Anthropology". Ed. Maurice Bloch. ASA Studies. Malaby Press. London, 1975.

Furnivall, J.S.: "Netherlands India: A Study of Plural Economy." Cambridge University Press. London. 1939.

Frank, Andre Gunder.: "Capitalism and Underdevelopment in Latin America." Modern Reader. New York. 1967.

Freed, Morton.: "On the Evolution Social Stratification and the State." In Culture and History: Essays in Honor of Paul Hodin. Stanley Diamond, ed. 1960. New York; Columbia University Press.

Gait, E.A.: "History of Assam." 3rd Rev. Ed'n. Thackey Spink. Calcutta 1967.

Ganguly, Milada: "Glimpses in Nagaland." 1984.

Gerth and Mills.: "From Max Weber". Routledge and Kegan Paul. London. 1948.

Giddens, Anthony.: "The Class Structure of Advanced Societies." Hutchinson and Co. London. 1973.

Godelier, Maurice.: "Rationality and Irrationality in Economics." Monthly Review Press. New York and London. 1972.

------------: "Perspectives in Marxist Anthropology" Cambridge University Press. London. 1977.

Goddard, David.: "Anthropology: Limits to Functionalism." From "Ideology in Social Sciences." Ed. Robin Blackburn Fontana. 1972.

Guha, Amalendu.: "Little Nationalism Turned Chauvanistic." Economic and Political Weekly. February, April and May. 1981.

Gundevia, Y.D.: "War and Peace in Nagaland." Palit and Palit Publishers. Dehra Dun. 1975.

Gutkind, Peter and : "African Social Studies." A Radical Reader Monthly Review Waterman, Peter. Ed. Press. New York. 1977.

Haimendorf, Christoph Von: "The Konyak Nagas." Holt and Rinehart. London.1969. Fuhrer.

Celia, S. Heller.: "Structured Social Inequality." Collier and Macmillan. London. 1969.

Heeger, A. Gerald.: "The Politics of Underdevelopment." Macmillan. London. 1974.

Horam, M.: "Naga Polity." B.R. Publishing Corporation. Delhi. 1975.

Hobsbawn, E.J.: "Karl Marx, Pre-Capitalist Economic Formation" Lawrence and Wishart Ltd. London. 1964.

Hurrell, Andrew and: "Inequality, Globalization and World Politics." Oxford Woods, Ngaire. University Press, New York 1999.

Hutchinson, John and Smith,: "Ethnicity." Oxford University Press, New York 1996. Anthony D.ED

Hutton, J.H.: "The Sema Nagas." Oxford University Press. London. 1921.

Hutton, J.H.: " The Angami Nagas." Oxford University Press. London 1926.

Huntington, Samuel P.: "Political Order in Changing Societies." Vakils, Fiffer and Simons Pvt. Ltd. , Bombay. 1968.

Imchen, Panger.: "Ancient Ao-Naga Religion and Culture". 1993, Har-Anand Publications New Delhi.

Jamir, Imliyanger K.: "Naga Insurgency: A Study" 1993. Tuli, Nagaland.

Keiusinen,O.: "Marxism and Leninism." Moscow Publishers 1961.

Kosambi, D.D.: "An Introduction to the History of Indian Society." Popular Prakashan. Bombay. 1975.

Kupuswamy, B.: "Social Change in India." Vikas. Delhi. 1972.

Leach, E.R.: "Political Systems of Highland Burma: A Study of Kachin Social Structure." London 1964.

Littlejohn, James.: "Social Stratification". Allen and Unwin. London 1972.

Luthra, P.N.: "Nagaland from a district to a state." Directorate of Information and Publicity. Arunachal Pradesh, Shillong, 1974.

Marx, Karl. : "Theories of Surplus Value." Moscow Publishers. 1962.

Marx, Karl and Engels, : "The German Ideology." 1864. Moscow Publishers. Reprint. Friederich. 1962.

Mathur, P.C. : "Regionalism in India." From "Regionalism in South-East Asia." Ed. Ramakant. Aalikh Publishers. 1983.

Mandelbaum, David.: "Society in India." Popular Prakashan. Bombay. 1970.

Mannheim, Karl.: "Essays on the Sociology of Culture." Routledge and Kegan Paul. London. 1956.

Misra, Udayon: "Naga Middle Class and Nationalism." From "The Emergence and Role of the Middle Class in North-East India." Ed. B. Datta Roy. Upal Publishing House. Delhi. 1983.

Misra, Bani Prassana.: "Kirata Karyo Kineses: An Introduction to the Political Economy of Tribal Societies in North-East India." From "Economics of the Tribes and their Transformation." Ed. K.S. Singh. Concept Publishing Company. New Delhi. 1982.

Mills, C. Wright.: "The Power Elite." Oxford University Press. New York. 1956.

------------: "The Middle Class in Middle Sized Cities." From "Class, Status and Power." Ed. Rhienhard Bendix and S.M. Lipset. IInd. Ed'n. Routledge and Kegan Paul. 1967.

Michell, St.John.: "The North-East Frontier of India (A Topographical, Political and Military Report)". Vivek Publishing House. Delhi. 1976.

Mills, J.P.: "The Lotha Nagas." Reprint 1996.

Mills, J.P. : "The Ao Nagas." Oxford University Press. London. 1921.

------------: "The Lotha Nagas (Second edition) Directorate of Art and Culture, Government of Nagaland 1980. (reprint)

Mills, B.B.: "The Indian Middle Class." Oxford University Press. London. 1961.

Miri, Sujata. Ed: "Religion in North-East India." Vikas Publishing House Pvt. Ltd. New Delhi. 1980.

Moasosang, P.: "Education and Social Change with Particular Reference to Nagaland." The Thinker Bulletin. Kohima 1974.

Neibor, H.J. : "Slavery as an Industrial System." The Hague. Nej Holf. 1960.

Ossowski, Stanislaw.: "Class Structure in the Social Consciousness." Harper and Row. London. 1963.

Osterbag, Dag.: "On Significance of Materialism in Sociology with reference to theories of Social Class." International Journal of Sociology. Winter 1979-80.

Organski, A.F.K.: "The Stages of Political Development." New York. 1965.

Parsons, Talcott.: "Essays on Sociological Theory." Revised Light and Life Publishers. 1975.

Parkins, Frank.: "Class Inequality and the Political Order." New York. 1971.

Peseyie, Kevinuno.: "Educational Development and Social Change in Nagaland." Highlander Bulletin. Kohima.1974.

Press, Erwin and Smith,: "Urban Place and Process". Readings in the Anthropology of Estellie M. Ed. Cities. Unwin. New York. 1974.

Panda, C.R.: "Imperialism and the Process of Colonization of the North-Eastern Region with Reference to the Naga Hills (1830-1910)". Seminar Paper. North-Eastern Hill University, Shillong. 1978.

Pareto, Vilfredo.: "The Mind and Society." Vol.3. Para 2027-31. London 1935.

Philips, P.T.: "The Growth of Baptist Church in Nagaland." Christian Literature Centre. Gauhati. 1983.

Ramuny, Murkot: "The World of Nagas." Northern Book Centre, New Delhi 1988.

Rao, Venkata.: "A Century of Tribal Politics." Delhi 1976. S. Chand and Company Ltd., Ram Nagar. New Delhi 1976.

Ross, Lola Ramucci & Devos,George.ED: "Ethnic Identity: Creation Conflict and Accomodation". Altamira Press. New Delhi 1995.

Rustumji, Nari.: "Imperilled Frontiers: India's North-Eastern Borderlands." Oxford University Press. Delhi 1983.

Smith, W.C.: "The Ao Naga Tribes of Assam." Gian Publications. Delhi 1980.

Stearns, Peter N.: "The Middle Class: Toward a Precise Definition ." Comparative

Studies in Study and History. Vol. 21. No.3, July 1979. Cambridge University Press.

Sherman, P. and Wood,: "Sociology: Traditional and Radical Perspectives." Harper and James L.Row Publishers. London 1982.

Sinha, A.C.: "Politics of Sikkim." Thomson Press Limited. 1975.

Somjee, A.H.: "Political Capacity in Developing Societies." Macmillan Press. Hong Kong. 1982.

Srinivas, M.N.: "Social Change in Modern India." Delhi 1972.

Tajenyuba: "A History of Anglo Naga Affairs." Gauhati 1958.

Terray, Emmanuel: "Class Consciousness and Development." From Marxist Analysis and Social Anthropology." Ed. Maurice Bloch. ASA Studies. Malaby Press. London. 1975.

Thakur, R.N.: "Elite Theory and Administrative Systems." Sterling Publishers. New Delhi. 1981.

Thomas, M.M.: "The Nagas Towards AD 2000." Selected addresses and writings; Centre for Research on New International Economic Order, Madras.1992

Thurnwald, Richard : "Economics in Primitive Communities." Oxford University Press. London 1932.

Tumin, Melvin M.: "Social Stratification. The Forms and Functions of SocialInequality." Prentice Hall. New York 1978.

United Nations Background: "The Role of Social Factors in Development." No.2 1969. Paper.Stockholm.

Veblen, Thorstein. : "The Theory of Leisure Class." Viking Press. New York 1931

Verghe,Van Den P.L.: "Ethnicity and Class in Highland Peru." From "Ethnicity and Resource Competition in Plural Societies." Ed. Leo A. Despres. Mouton Publishers.Paris.1975

Warner, Lloyd and: "The Social Life of a Modern Community-New Haven." Viking Lunt, P.S. Press. New York. 1941.

Yaden, L.L.: "Nagaland." Laxmi Press. New Delhi. 1970.

Yinger, Milton J.: "Ethnicity: Sources of Strength? Source of Conflict? 1997. Ranat Publications. New Delhi.

Yonuo, Asoso.: "The Rising Nagas." Vikas. Delhi 1974.

SELECT OFFICIAL SOURCES

1. Sub-Divisional Office Record (Abstract) 1889. Mokokchung.
2. Deputy Commissioner, Office Record (Abstract) 1957. Mokokchung.
3. Statistical Handbook of Nagaland, 2000, Millenium Issue.
4. Statistical Handbook of Nagaland, 2001.
5. Directorate of Food and Civil Supplies, 2002, Dimapur.
6. Town Planning Organization, Mokokchung. Urban Plan Report 2002.
7. Mokokchung Town Committee, Annual Report, 2001.
8. Nagaland Annual, 2000, DIPR, Kohima.
9. Nagaland (1993-2002) A Decade of Stability, Progress and Development DIPR, Kohima.
10. Nagaland Basic Facts, 2002, DIPR, Kohima.
11. India 2003, Observer Statistical Handbook, Observer Research Foundation, New Delhi.
12. Basic Statistics of North-Eastern Region, 1995 and 2000. North-Eastern Council, Ministry of Home Affairs, Government of India.

[1] In this study, the term like Nagas, Naga tribes, Naga tribal groups, Naga tribesmen and tribals are used interchangeably. It may be noted that they all refer to the tribal inhabitants of the then Naga Hills District constituted in 1866 and later of the state of Nagaland today.

INDEX

S

T

□□□